FARM LEGENDS.

FARM LEGENDS

By WILL CARLETON

AUTHOR OF "FARM BALLADS"

ILLUSTRATED

NEW YORK

HARPER & BROTHERS, PUBLISHERS

FRANKLIN SQUARE

1876

2298

TO

THE MEMORY OF A NOBLEMAN,

MY

FARMER FATHER.

PREFACE.

The "Farm Ballads" have met with so kind and general a reception as to encourage the publishing of a companion volume.

In this book, also, the author has aimed to give expression to the truth, that with every person, even if humble or debased, there may be some good, worth lifting up and saving; that in each human being, though revered and seemingly immaculate, are some faults which deserve pointing out and correcting; and that all circumstances of life, however trivial they appear, may possess those alternations of the comic and pathetic, the good and bad, the joyful and sorrowful, upon which walk the days and nights, the summers and winters, the lives and deaths, of this strange world.

He would take this occasion to give a word of thanks to those who have staid with him through evil and good report; who have overlooked his literary faults for the sake of the truths he was struggling to tell; and who have believed—what he knows—that he is honest.

With these few words of introduction, the author launches this second bark upon the sea of popular opinion; grinds his axe, and enters once more the great forest of Human Nature, for timber to go on with his boat-building.

W. C.

CONTENTS.

FARM LEGENDS.

OTHER POEMS.

ILLUSTRATIONS.

—⊲◆⊳—

FARM LEGENDS.

FARM LEGENDS.

THE SCHOOL-MASTER'S GUESTS.

I.

THE district school-master was sitting behind his great book-laden desk,
Close-watching the motions of scholars, pathetic and gay and grotesque.

As whisper the half-leafless branches, when Autumn's brisk breezes have
come,
His little scrub-thicket of pupils sent upward a half-smothered hum.

Like the frequent sharp bang of a wagon, when treading a forest path o'er,
Resounded the feet of his pupils, whenever their heels struck the floor.

There was little Tom Timms on the front seat, whose face was with-
standing a drouth;
And jolly Jack Gibbs just behind him, with a rainy new moon for a
mouth.

There were both of the Smith boys, as studious as if they bore names
that could bloom;
And Jim Jones, a heaven-built mechanic, the slyest young knave in the
room,

With a countenance grave as a horse's, and his honest eyes fixed on a
pin,
Queer-bent on a deeply laid project to tunnel Joe Hawkins's skin.

2

There were anxious young novices, drilling their spelling-books into the
brain,
Loud-puffing each half-whispered letter, like an engine just starting its
train.

There was one fiercely muscular fellow, who scowled at the sums on his
slate,
And leered at the innocent figures a look of unspeakable hate,

And set his white teeth close together, and gave his thin lips a short
twist,
As to say, "I could whip you, confound you! could such things be
done with the fist!"

There were two knowing girls in the corner, each one with some beauty
possessed,
In a whisper discussing the problem which one the young master likes
best.

A class in the front, with their readers, were telling, with difficult pains,
How perished brave Marco Bozzaris while bleeding at all of his veins;

And a boy on the floor to be punished, a statue of idleness stood,
Making faces at all of the others, and enjoying the scene all he could.

II.

Around were the walls gray and dingy, which every old school-sanctum
hath,
With many a break on their surface, where grinned a wood-grating of
lath.

A patch of thick plaster, just over the school-master's rickety chair,
Seemed threat'ningly o'er him suspended, like Damocles' sword, by a hair.

There were tracks on the desks where the knife-blades had wandered
in search of their prey ;
Their tops were as duskily spattered as if they drank ink every day.

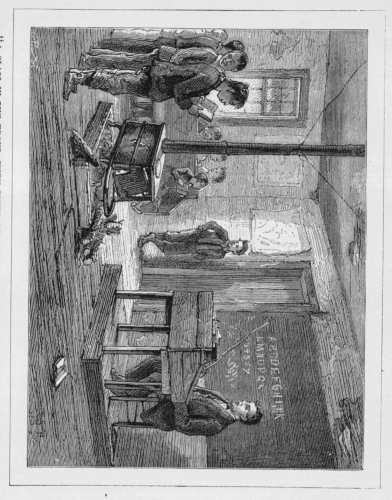

"A CLASS IN THE FRONT, WITH THEIR READERS, WERE TELLING, WITH DIFFICULT PAINS,
HOW PERISHED BRAVE MARCO BOZZARIS WHILE BLEEDING AT ALL OF HIS VEINS."

The square stove it puffed and it crackled, and broke out in red-flaming
    sores,
Till the great iron quadruped trembled like a dog fierce to rush out-o'-
    doors.

White snow-flakes looked in at the windows; the gale pressed its lips to
    the cracks;
And the children's hot faces were streaming, the while they were freezing
    their backs.

III.

Now Marco Bozzaris had fallen, and all of his suff'rings were o'er,
And the class to their seats were retreating, when footsteps were heard
    at the door;

And five of the good district fathers marched into the room in a row,
And stood themselves up by the hot fire, and shook off their white
    cloaks of snow;

And the spokesman, a grave squire of sixty, with countenance solemnly
    sad,
Spoke thus, while the children all listened, with all of the ears that they
    had:

" We've come here, school-master, intendin' to cast an inquirin' eye
    'round,
Concernin' complaints that's been entered, an' fault that has lately been
    found;
To pace off the width of your doin's, an' witness what you've been about,
An' see if it's payin' to keep you, or whether we'd best turn ye out.

" The first thing I'm bid for to mention is, when the class gets up to
    read,
You give 'em too tight of a reinin', an' touch 'em up more than they need;
You're nicer than wise in the matter of holdin' the book in one han',
An' you turn a stray *g* in their doin's, an' tack an odd *d* on their *an'*.
There ain't no great good comes of speakin' the words so *polite*, as *I* see,
Providin' you know what the facts is, an' tell 'em off jest as they be.

An' then there's that readin' in corncert, is censured from first unto
　　last;
It kicks up a heap of a racket, when folks is a-travelin' past.
Whatever is done as to readin', providin' things go to *my* say,
Sha'n't hang on no new-fangled hinges, but swing in the old-fashioned
　　way."

And the other four good district fathers gave quick the consent that was
　　due,
And nodded obliquely, and muttered, " *Them 'ere is my sentiments tew.*"

" Then, as to your spellin': I've heern tell, by them as has looked into
　　this,
That you turn the *u* out o' your labour, an' make the word shorter than
　　'tis;
An' clip the *k* off o' yer musick, which makes my son Ephraim perplexed,
An' when he spells out as he ought'r, you pass the word on to the
　　next.
They say there's some new-grafted books here that don't take them letters
　　along;
But if it is so, just depend on't, them new-grafted books is made wrong.
You might just as well say that Jackson didn't know all there was about
　　war,
As to say that old Spellin'-book Webster didn't know what them letters
　　was for."

And the other four good district fathers gave quick the consent that was
　　due,
And scratched their heads slyly and softly, and said, " *Them's my
　　sentiments tew.*"

" Then, also, your 'rithmetic doin's, as they are reported to me,
Is that you have left Tare an' Tret out, an' also the old Rule o' Three;
An' likewise brought in a new study, some high-steppin' scholars to
　　please,
With saw-bucks an' crosses and pot-hooks, an' *w*'s, *x*, *y*'s, and *z*'s.
We ain't got no time for such foolin'; there ain't no great good to be
　　reached
By tiptoein' childr'n up higher than ever their fathers was teached."

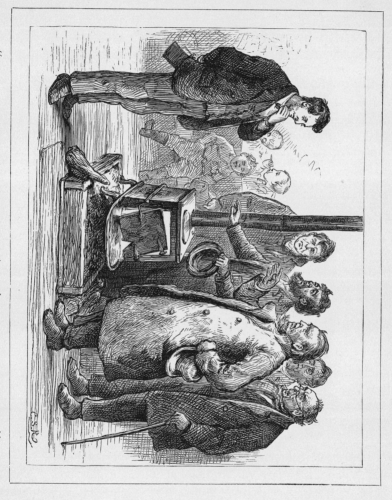

"AND NODDED OBLIQUELY, AND MUTTERED, 'THEM 'ERE IS MY SENTIMENTS TEW.'"

And the other four good district fathers gave quick the consent that was
  due,
And cocked one eye up to the ceiling, and said, " *Them's my sentiments tew.*"

"Another thing, I must here mention, comes into the question to-day,
Concernin' some things in the grammar you're teachin' our gals for to say.
My gals is as steady as clock-work, an' never give cause for much fear,
But they come home from school t'other evenin' a-talkin' such stuff as
  this here :
'*I love,*' an' '*Thou lovest,*' an' '*He loves,*' an' '*Ye love,*' an' '*You love,*' an'
  '*They—*'
An' they answered my questions, 'It's grammar'—'twas all I could get
  'em to say.
Now if, 'stead of doin' your duty, you're carryin' matters on so
As to make the gals say that they love you, it's just all that *I* want to
  know ;—"

IV.

Now Jim, the young heaven-built mechanic, in the dusk of the evening
  before,
Had well-nigh unjointed the stove-pipe, to make it come down on the
  floor ;

And the squire bringing smartly his foot down, as a clincher to what he
  had said,
A joint of the pipe fell upon him, and larruped him square on the head.

The soot flew in clouds all about him, and blotted with black all the place,
And the squire and the other four fathers were peppered with black in
  the face.

The school, ever sharp for amusement, laid down all their cumbersome
  books,
And, spite of the teacher's endeavors, laughed loud at their visitors' looks.

And the squire, as he stalked to the doorway, swore oaths of a violet hue;
And the four district fathers, who followed, seemed to say, " *Them's my
  sentiments tew.*"

THREE LINKS OF A LIFE.

I.

A WORD went over the hills and plains
Of the scarce-hewn fields that the Tiffin drains,
Through dens of swamps and jungles of trees,
As if it were borne by the buzzing bees
As something sweet for the sons of men;
Or as if the blackbird and the wren
Had lounged about each ragged clearing
To gossip it in the settlers' hearing;
Or the partridge drum-corps of the wood
Had made the word by mortals heard,
And Diana made it understood;
Or the loud-billed hawk of giant sweep
Were told it as something he must keep;

As now, in the half-built city of Lane,
Where the sons of the settlers strive for gain,
Where the Indian trail is graded well,
And the anxious ring of the engine-bell
And the Samson Steam's deep, stuttering word
And the factory's dinner-horn are heard;
Where burghers fight, in friendly guise,
With spears of bargains and shields of lies;
Where the sun-smoked farmer, early a-road,
Rides into the town his high-built load
Of wood or wool, or corn or wheat,
And stables his horses in the street;—
It seems as to each and every one
A deed were known ere it well be done,

"WHEN GRAVE BAW BEESE, THE INDIAN CHIEF,
HAD BEADED THE NECK OF THE PALE-FACE MISS."

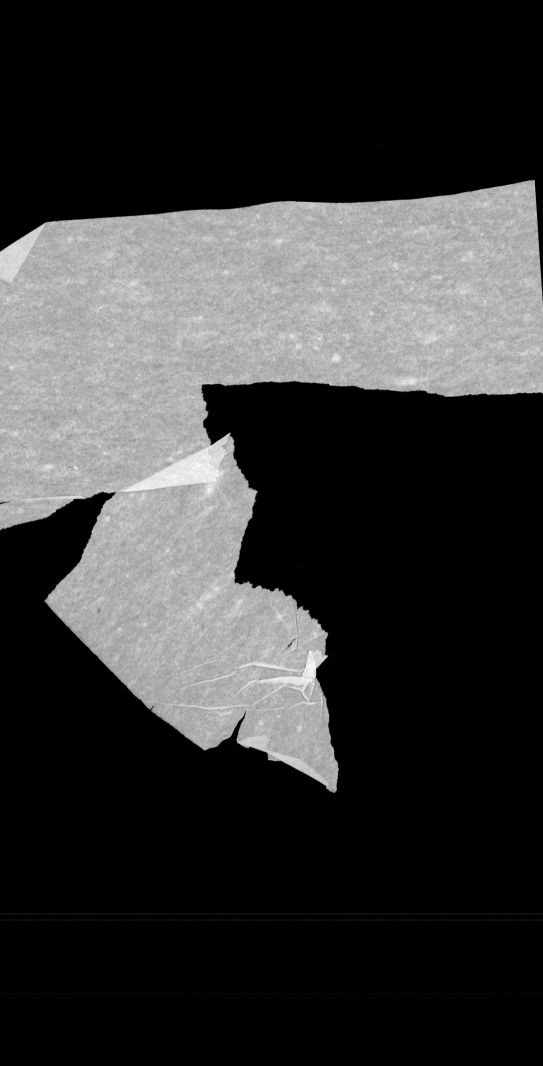

As if, in spite of roads or weather,
All minds were whispering together;
So over the glens and rough hill-sides
Of the fruitful land where the Tiffin glides,
Went the startling whisper, clear and plain,
" *There's a new-born baby over at Lane!*"

Now any time, from night till morn,
Or morn till night, for a long time-flight,
Had the patient squaws their children borne;
And many a callow, coppery wight
Had oped his eyes to the tree-flecked light,
And grown to the depths of the woodland dell
And the hunt of the toilsome hills as well
As though at his soul a bow were slung,
And a war-whoop tattooed on his tongue;
But never before, in the Tiffin's sight,
Had a travail bloomed with a blossom of white.

And the fire-tanned logger no longer pressed
His yoke-bound steeds and his furnace fire;
And the gray-linked log-chain drooped to rest,
And a hard face softened with sweet desire;
And the settler-housewife, rudely wise,
With the forest's shrewdness in her eyes,
Yearned, with tenderly wondering brain,
For the new-born baby over at Lane.

And the mother lay in her languid bed,
When the flock of visitors had fled—
When the crowd of settlers all had gone,
And left the young lioness alone
With the tiny cub they had come to see
In the rude-built log menagerie;
When grave Baw Beese, the Indian chief,
As courtly as ever prince in his prime,
Or cavalier of the olden time,
Making his visit kind as brief,
Had beaded the neck of the pale-face miss,

And dimpled her cheek with a farewell kiss;
When the rough-clad room was still as sleek,
Save the deaf old nurse's needle-click,
The beat of the grave clock in its place,
With its ball-tipped tail and owl-like face,
And the iron tea-kettle's droning song
Through its Roman nose so black and long,
The mother lifted her baby's head,
And gave it a clinging kiss, and said:

Why did thou come so straight to me,
    Thou queer one?
Thou might have gone where riches be,
    Thou dear one!
For when 'twas talked about in heaven,
To whom the sweet soul should be given,
If thou had raised thy pretty voice,
God sure had given to thee a choice,
    My dear one, my queer one!

"Babe in the wood" thou surely art,
    My lone one:
But thou shalt never play the part,
    My own one!
Thou ne'er shalt wander up and down,
With none to claim thee as their own;
Nor shall the Redbreast, as she grieves,
Make up for thee a bed of leaves,
    My own one, my lone one!

Although thou be not Riches' flower,
    Thou neat one,
Yet thou hast come from Beauty's bower,
    Thou sweet one!
Thy every smile's as warm and bright
As if a diamond mocked its light;
Thy every tear's as pure a pearl
As if thy father was an earl,
    Thou neat one, thou sweet one!

And thou shalt have a queenly name,
    Thou grand one:
A lassie's christening's half her fame,
    Thou bland one!
And may thou live so good and true,
The honor will but be thy due;
And friends shall never be ashamed,
Or when or where they hear thee named,
    Thou bland one, thou grand one!

E'en like the air—our rule and sport—
    Thou meek one,
Thou art my burden and support,
    Thou weak one!
Like manna in the wilderness,
A joy hath come to soothe and bless;
But 'tis a sorrow unto me,
To love as I am loving thee,
    Thou weak one, thou meek one!

The scarlet-coated child-thief waits,
    Thou bright one,
To bear thee through the sky-blue gates,
    Thou light one!
His feverish touch thy brow may pain,
And while I to my sad lips strain
The sheath of these bright-beaming eyes,
The blade may flash back to the skies,
    Thou light one, thou bright one!

And if thou breast the morning storm,
    Thou fair one,
And gird a woman's thrilling form,
    Thou rare one:
Sly hounds of sin thy path will trace,
And on thy unsuspecting face
Hot lust will rest its tarnished eyes,
And thou wilt need be worldly-wise,
    Thou rare one, thou fair one!

O that the heaven that smiles to-day,
    My blest one,
May give thee light to see thy way,
    My best one!
That when around thee creeps The Gloom,
The gracious God will call thee home,
And then, increased a hundredfold,
Thou proudly hand Him back His gold,
My best one, my blest one!

II.

A word went over the many miles
Of the well-tilled land where the Tiffin smiles,
And sought no youthful ear in vain:
" *There's a wedding a-coming off at Lane!*"

They stood in the shade of the western door—
Father, mother, and daughter one—
And gazed, as they oft had gazed before,
At the downward glide of the western sun.
The rays of his never-jealous light
Made even the cloud that dimmed him bright;
And lower he bent, and kissed, as he stood,
The lips of the distant blue-eyed wood.

And just as the tired sun bowed his head,
The sun-browned farmer sighed, and said:

    And so you'll soon be goin' away,
      My darling little Bess;
    And you ha' been to the store to-day,
      To buy your weddin'-dress;

    And so your dear good mother an' I,
      Whose love you long have known,
    Must lay the light o' your presence by,
      And walk the road alone.

So come to-night, with mother and me,
    To the porch for an hour or two,
And sit on your old father's knee,
    The same as you used to do;

For we, who ha' loved you many a year,
    And clung to you, strong and true,
Since we've had the young Professor here,
    Have not had much of you!

But lovers be lovers while earth endures;
    And once on a time, be it known,
I helped a girl with eyes like yours
    Construct a world of our own;

And we laid it out in a garden spot,
    And dwelt in the midst of flowers,
Till we found that the world was a good-sized lot,
    And most of it wasn't ours!

You're heavier, girl, than when you come
    To us one cloudy day,
And seemed to feel so little at home,
    We feared you wouldn't stay;

Till I knew the danger was passed, because
    You'd struck so mortal a track,
And got so independent an' cross,
    God never would let you back!

But who would ever ha' had the whim,
    When you lay in my arms an' cried,
You'd some time sit here, pretty an' prim,
    A-waitin' to be a bride!

But lovers be lovers while earth goes on,
    And marry, as they ought;
And if you would keep the heart you've won,
    Remember what you've been taught:

3

Look first that your wedded lives be true,
  With naught from each other apart;
For the flowers of true love never grew
  In the soil of a faithless heart.

Look next that the buds of health shall rest
  Their blossoms upon your cheek;
For life and love are a burden at best
  If the body be sick and weak.

Look next that your kitchen fire be bright,
  And your hands be neat and skilled;
For the love of man oft takes its flight
  If his stomach be not well filled.

Look next that your money is fairly earned
  Ere ever it be spent;
For comfort and love, however turned,
  Will ne'er pay ten per cent.

And, next, due care and diligence keep
  That the mind be trained and fed;
For blessings ever look shabby and cheap
  That light on an empty head.

And if it shall please the gracious God
  That children to you belong,
Remember, my child, and spare the rod
  Till you've taught them right and wrong;

And show 'em that though this life's a start
  For the better world, no doubt,
Yet earth an' heaven ain't so far apart
  As many good folks make out.

III.

A word went over the broad hill-sweeps
Of the listening land where the Tiffin creeps:

"*She married, holding on high her head;*
But the groom was false as the vows he said;
With lies and crimes his days are checked;
The girl is alone, and her life is wrecked."

The midnight rested its heavy arm
Upon the grief-encumbered farm;
And hoarse-voiced Sorrow wandered at will,
Like a moan when the summer's night is still;

"HIDING E'EN FROM THE DARK HIS FACE."

And the spotted cows, with bellies of white,
And well-filled teats all crowded awry,
Stood in the black stalls of the night,
Nor herded nor milked, and wondered why.
And the house was gloomy, still, and cold;
And the hard-palmed farmer, newly old,
Sat in an unfrequented place,
Hiding e'en from the dark his face;
And a solemn silence rested long
On all, save the cricket's dismal song.

But the mother drew the girl to her breast,
And gave to her spirit words of rest:

Come to my lap, my wee-grown baby; rest thee upon my knee;
You have been traveling toward the light, and drawing away from me;
You turned your face from my dark path to catch the light o' the sun,
And 'tis no more nor less, my child, than children ever have done.
So you joined hands with one you loved, when we to the cross-road
        came,
And went your way, as Heaven did say, and who but Heaven to
        blame?

You must not weep that he you chose was all the time untrue,
Or stab with hate the man whose heart you thought was made for you.
The love God holds for your bright soul is more to get and give
Than all the love of all of the men while He may bid them live.
So let your innocence stanch the wound made by another's guilt;
For Vengeance' blade was ever made with neither guard nor hilt.

Who will avenge you, darling? The sun that shines on high.
He will paint the picture of your wrongs before the great world's eye.
He will look upon your sweet soul, in its pure mantle of white,
Till it shine upon your enemies, and dazzle all their sight.
He'll come each day to point his finger at him who played the knave;
And 'tis denied from him to hide, excepting in the grave.

Who will avenge you, darling? Your sister, the sky above.
Each cloud she floats above you shall be a token of love;
She will bend o'er you at night-fall her pure broad breast of blue,
And every gem that glitters there shall flash a smile to you.
And all her great wide distances to your good name belong;
'Tis not so far from star to star as 'twixt the right and wrong.

Who will avenge you, darling? All the breezes that blow.
They will whisper to each other your tale of guiltless woe;
The perfumes that do load them your innocence shall bless,
And they will soothe your aching brow with pitying, kind caress.
They will sweep away the black veil that hangs about your fame:
There is no cloud that long can shroud a virtuous woman's name.

Who will avenge you, darling? The one who proved untrue.
His memory must undo him, whate'er his will may do;

"E'EN IN YOUR DESOLATION YOU ARE NOT QUITE UNBLEST:
NOT ALL WHO CHOOSE MAY COUNT THEIR WOES UPON A MOTHER'S BREAST."

The pitch-black night will come when he must meet Remorse alone;
He will rush at your avenging as if it were his own.
His every sin is but a knot that yet shall hold him fast;
For guilty hands but twine the strands that fetter them at last.

Lay thee aside thy grief, darling!—lay thee aside thy grief!
And Happiness will cheer thee beyond all thy belief!
As oft as winter comes summer, as sure as night comes day,
And as swift as sorrow cometh, so swift it goeth away!
E'en in your desolation you are not quite unblest:
Not all who choose may count their woes upon a mother's breast.

ROB, THE PAUPER.

I.

ROB, the Pauper, is loose again.
    Through the fields and woods he races.
He shuns the women, he beats the men,
    He kisses the children's frightened faces.
There is no mother he hath not fretted;
There is no child he hath not petted;
There is no house, by road or lane,
He did not tap at the window-pane,
And make more dark the dismal night,
And set the faces within with white.

Rob, the Pauper, is wild of eye,
    Wild of speech, and wild of thinking;
Over his forehead broad and high,
    Each with each wild locks are linking.
Yet there is something in his bearing
Not quite what a pauper should be wearing:
In every step is a shadow of grace;
The ghost of a beauty haunts his face;
The rags half-sheltering him to-day
Hang not on him in a beggarly way.

Rob, the Pauper, is crazed of brain:
    The world is a lie to his shattered seeming.
No woman is true unless insane;
    No man but is full of lecherous scheming.
Woe to the wretch, of whate'er calling,
That crouches beneath his cudgel's falling!
Pity the wife, howe'er high-born,
Who wilts beneath his words of scorn!
But youngsters he caresses as wild
As a mother would kiss a rescued child.

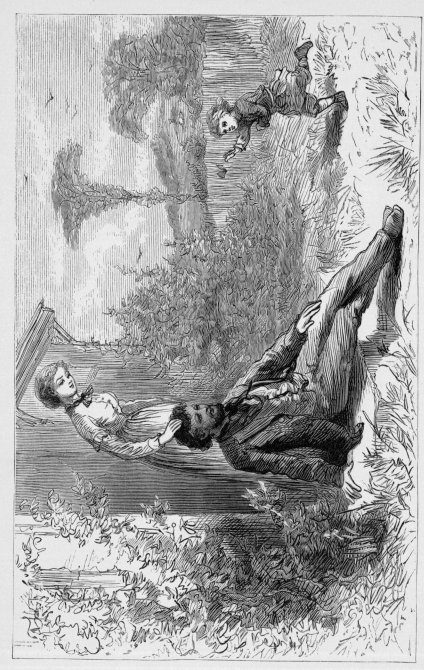

"HIMSELF ON THE DOOR-STONE IDLY SITTING,
A BLONDE-HAIRED WOMAN ABOUT HIM FLITTING."

He hath broke him loose from his poor-house cell;
   He hath dragged him clear from rope and fetter.
They might have thought; for they know full well
   They could keep a half-caged panther better.
Few are the knots so strategy-shunning
That they can escape his maniac cunning;
Many a stout bolt strives in vain
To bar his brawny shoulders' strain;
The strongest men in town agree
That the Pauper is good for any three.

He hath crossed the fields, the woods, the street;
   He hides in the swamp his wasted feature;
The frog leaps over his bleeding feet;
   The turtle crawls from the frightful creature.
The loud mosquito, hungry-flying,
For his impoverished blood is crying;
The scornful hawk's loud screaming sneer
Falls painfully upon his ear;
And close to his unstartled eye
The rattlesnake creeps noisily by.

He hath fallen into a slough of sleep.
   A haze of the past bends softly o'er him.
His restless spirit a watch doth keep,
   As Memory's canvas glides before him.
Through slumber's distances he travels;
The tangled skein of his mind unravels;
The bright past dawns through a cloud of dreams,
And once again in his prime he seems;
For over his heart's lips, as a kiss,
Sweepeth a vision like to this:

A cozy kitchen, a smooth-cut lawn,
   A zephyr of flowers in the bright air straying;
A graceful child, as fresh as dawn,
   Upon the greensward blithely playing;
Himself on the door-stone idly sitting,
A blonde-haired woman about him flitting.

She fondly stands beside him there,
And deftly toys with his coal-black hair,
And hovers about him with her eyes,
And whispers to him, pleading-wise :

O Rob, why will you plague my heart? why will you try me so?
　Is she so fair, is she so sweet, that you must need desert me?
I saw you kiss her twice and thrice behind the maple row,
　And each caress you gave to her did like a dagger hurt me.
Why should for her and for her smiles your heart a moment hunger?
What though her shape be trim as mine, her face a trifle younger?
She does not look so young to you as I when we were wed;
She can not speak more sweet to you than words that I have said;
She can not love you half so well as I, when all is done;
And she is not your wedded wife—the mother of your son.

O Rob, you smile and toss your head; you mock me in your soul;
　You say I would be overwise—that I am jealous of you;
And what if my tight-bended heart should spring beyond control?
　My jealous tongue but tells the more the zeal with which I love you.
Oh, we might be so peaceful here, with nothing of reproving!
Oh, we might be so happy here, with none to spoil our loving!
Why should a joy be more a joy because, forsooth, 'tis hid?
How can a kiss be more a kiss because it is forbid?
Why should the love you get from her be counted so much gain,
When every smile you give to her but adds unto my pain?

O Rob, you say there is no guilt betwixt the girl and you :
　Do you not know how slack of vows may break the bond that's
　　dearest?
You twirl a plaything in your hand, not minding what you do,
　And first you know it flies from you, and strikes the one that's
　　nearest.
So do not spoil so hopelessly you ne'er may cease your ruing;
The finger-post of weakened vows points only to undoing.
Remember there are years to come, and there are thorns of woe
That you may grasp if once you let the flowers of true love go.
Remember the increasing bliss of marriage undefiled;
Remember all the pride or shame that waits for yonder child!

"HE RUNS AND STUMBLES, LEAPS AND CLAMBERS,
THROUGH THE DENSE THICKET'S BREATHLESS CHAMBERS."

II.

Rob, the Pauper, awakes and runs;
   A clamor cometh clear and clearer.
They are hunting him with dogs and guns;
   They are every moment pressing nearer.
Through pits of stagnant pools he pushes,
Through the thick sumac's poison bushes;
He runs and stumbles, leaps and clambers,
Through the dense thicket's breathless chambers.
The swamp-slime stains at his bloody tread;
The tamarack branches rasp his head.

From bog to bog, and from slough to slough,
   He flees, but his foes come yelling nearer;
And ever unto his senses now
   The long-drawn bay of the hounds is clearer.
He is worn and worried, hot and panting;
He staggers at every footstep's planting;
The hot blood races through his brain;
His every breath is a twinge of pain;
Black shadows dance before his eyes;
The echoes mock his agony-cries.

They have hunted him to the open field;
   He is falling upon their worn-out mercies.
They loudly call to him to yield;
   He hoarsely pays them back in curses.
His blood-shot eye is wildly roaming;
His firm-set mouth with rage is foaming;
He waves his cudgel, with war-cry loud,
And dares the bravest of the crowd.
There springs at his throat a hungry hound;
He dashes its brains into the ground.

Rob, the Pauper, is sorely pressed.
   The men are crowding all around him.
He crushes one to a bloody rest,
   And breaks again from the crowd that bound him.

The crash of a pistol comes unto him—
A well-sped ball goes crushing through him;
But still he rushes on—yet on—
Until, at last, some distance won,
He mounts a fence with a madman's ease,
And this is something of what he sees:

A lonely cottage, some tangled grass,
　　Thickets of thistles, dock, and mullein;
A forest of weeds he scarce can pass,
　　A broken chimney, cold and sullen;
Trim housewife-ants, with rush uncertain,
The spider hanging her gauzy curtain.
The Pauper falls on the dusty floor,
And there rings in his failing ear once more
　・　A voice as it might be from the dead,
And says, as it long ago hath said:

O Rob, I have a word to say—a cruel word—to you:
　I can not longer live a lie—the truth for air is calling!
I can not keep the secret locked that long has been your due,
　Not if you strike me to the ground, and spurn me in my falling!
He came to me when first a cloud across your smile was creeping—
He came to me—he brought to me a slighted heart for keeping;
He would not see my angry frown; he sought me, day by day;
I flung at him hot words of scorn, I turned my face away.
I bade him dread my husband's rage when once his words were known.
He smiled at me, and said I had no husband of my own!

O Rob, his words were overtrue! they burned into my brain!
　I could not rub them out again, were I awake or sleeping!
I saw you kiss her twice and thrice—my chidings were in vain—
　And well I knew your wayward heart had wandered from my keeping.
I counted all that was at stake—I bribed my pride with duty;
I knelt before your manly face, in worship of its beauty;
I painted pictures for your eyes you were too blind to see;
I worked at all the trades of love, to earn you back to me;
I threw myself upon your heart; I plead and prayed to stay;
I held my hands to you for help—you pushed them both away!

He came to me again; he held his eager love to me—
   To me, whose weak and hungry heart deep desolation dreaded!
And I had learned to pity him; but still my will was free,
   And once again I threatened him, and warned him I was wedded.
He bade me follow him, and see my erring fancy righted.
We crept along a garden glade by moonbeams dimly lighted;
She silent sat 'mid clustering vines, though much her eyes did speak,
And your black hair was tightly pressed unto her glowing cheek....
It crazed me, but he soothed me sweet with love's unnumbered charms;
I, desolate, turned and threw myself into his desolate arms!

O Rob, you know how little worth, when once a woman slips,
   May be the striking down a hand to save herself from falling!
Once more my heart groped for your heart, my tired lips sought your lips;
   But 'twas too late—'twas after dark—and you were past recalling.
'Tis hard to claim what once is given; my foe was unrelenting;
Vain were the tempests of my rage, the mists of my repenting.
The night was dark, the storm had come, the fancy-stars of youth
Were covered over by the thick unfading cloud of truth;
So one by one the stars went back, each hid its pale white face,
Till all was dark, and all was drear, and all was black disgrace.

O Rob, good-by; a solemn one!—'tis till the Judgment-day.
   You look about you for the boy? You never more shall see him.
He's crying for his father now full many miles away;
   For he is mine—you need not rage—you can not find or free him.
We might have been so peaceful here, with nothing of reproving—
We might have been so happy here, with none to spoil our loving—
As I, a guilty one, might kiss a corpse's waiting brow,
I bend to you where you have fallen, and calmly kiss you now;
As I, a wronged and injured one, might seek escape's glad door,
I wander forth into the world, to enter here no more.

III.

Rob, the Pauper, is lying in state.
   In a box of rough-planed boards, unpainted,
He waits at the poor-house grave-yard gate,
   For a home by human lust untainted.

4

They are crowding around and closely peering
At the face of the foe who is past their fearing;
The men lift children up to see
The arms of the man who was good for three;
The women gaze and hold their breath,
For the man looks kingly even in death.

They have gone to their homes anear and far—
   Their joys and griefs, their loves and hating;
Some to sunder the ties that are,
   And some to cooing and wooing and mating.
They will pet and strike, they will strive and blunder,
And leer at their woes with innocent wonder;
They will swiftly sail love's delicate bark,
With never a helm, in the dangerous dark;
They will ne'er quite get it understood
That the Pauper's woes were for their good.

THE THREE LOVERS.

HERE'S a precept, young man, you should follow with care:
If you're courting a girl, court her honest and square.

Mr. 'Liakim Smith was a hard-fisted farmer,
        Of moderate wealth,
        And immoderate health,
Who fifty-odd years, in a stub-and-twist armor
        Of callus and tan,
        Had fought like a man
His own dogged progress, through trials and cares,
And log-heaps and brush-heaps and wild-cats and bears,
And agues and fevers and thistles and briers,
Poor kinsmen, rich foemen, false saints, and true liars;
Who oft, like the "man in our town," overwise,
Through the brambles of error had scratched out his eyes,
And when the unwelcome result he had seen,
        Had altered his notion,
        Reversing the motion,
And scratched them both in again, perfect and clean;
Who had weathered some storms, as a sailor might say,
And tacked to the left and the right of his way,
Till he found himself anchored, past tempests and breakers,
Upon a good farm of a hundred-odd acres.

As for 'Liakim's wife, in four words may be told
        Her whole standing in life:
        She was 'Liakim's wife.
Whereas she'd been young, she was now growing old,
But did, she considered, as well as one could,
When HE looked on her hard work, and saw that 'twas good.

The family record showed only a daughter;
But she had a face,
As if each fabled Grace
In a burst of delight to her bosom had caught her,
Or as if all the flowers in each Smith generation
Had blossomed at last in one grand culmination.
Style lingered unconscious in all of her dresses;
She'd starlight for glances, and sunbeams for tresses.
Wherever she went, with her right royal tread,
Each youth, when he'd passed her a bit, turned his head;
And so one might say, though the figure be strained,
She had turned half the heads that the township contained.

Now Bess had a lover—a monstrous young hulk;
A farmer by trade—
Strong, sturdy, and staid;
A man of good parts—if you counted by bulk;
A man of great weight—by the scales; and, indeed,
A man of some depth—as was shown by his feed.
His face was a fat exclamation of wonder;
His voice was not quite unsuggestive of thunder;
His laugh was a cross 'twixt a yell and a chuckle;
He'd a number one foot,
And a number ten boot,
And a knock-down reserved in each separate knuckle.
He'd a heart mad in love with the girl of his choice,
Who made him alternately mope and rejoice,
By dealing him one day discouraging messes,
And soothing him next day with smiles and caresses.

Now Bess had a lover, who hoped her to wed—
A rising young lawyer—more rising than read;
Whose theories all were quite startling; and who,
Like many a chap
In these days of strange hap,
Was living on what he expected to do;
While his landlady thought 'twould have been rather neat
Could he only have learned,
Till some practice was earned,

To subsist upon what he expected to eat.
He was bodily small, howe'er mentally great,
And suggestively less than a hundred in weight.

Now Bess had a lover—young Patrick; a sinner,
        And lad of all work,
        From the suburbs of Cork,
Who worked for her father, and thought *he* could win her.
And if Jacob could faithful serve fourteen years through,
        And still thrive and rejoice,
        For the girl of his choice,
He thought he could play the same game one or two.

Now 'Liakim Smith had a theory hid,
        And by egotism fed,
        Somewhere up in his head,
That a dutiful daughter should always as bid
Grow old in the service of him who begot her,
        Imbibe his beliefs,
        Have a care for his griefs,
And faithfully bring him his cider and water.
So, as might be expected, he turned up his nose,
Also a cold shoulder, to Bessie's two beaux,
And finally turned them away from his door,
Forbidding them ever to enter it more;
And detailed young Patrick as kind of a guard,
With orders to keep them both out of the yard.
So Pat took his task, with a treacherous smile,
        And bullied the small one,
        And dodged the big tall one,
And slyly made love to Miss Bess all the while.

But one evening, when 'Liakim and wife crowned their labors
        With praise and entreating
        At the village prayer-meeting,
And Patrick had stepped for a while to some neighbor's,
The lawyer had come, in the trimmest of dress,
        And, dapper and slim,
        And small, e'en for him,

Was holding a session of court with Miss Bess.
And Bess, sly love-athlete, was suited first rate
At a flirtation-mill with this legal light-weight;
And was listening to him, as minutes spun on,
   Of pleas he could make,
   And of fees he would take,
And of suits that he should, in the future, have won;
When just as the cold, heartless clock counted eight,
Miss Bessie's quick ear caught a step at the gate.
"'Tis mother!" she cried: "oh, go quick, I implore!
But father 'll drive 'round and come in the back-door!
You can not escape them, however you turn!
So hide for a while—let me see—in this churn!"

The churn was quite large enough for him to turn in—
   Expanded out so,
   By machinery to go,
'Twould have done for a dairy-man-Cyclops to churn in.
'Twas fixed for attaching a pitman or lever,
To go by a horse-power—a notion quite clever,
Invented and built by the Irishman, Pat,
Who pleased Mrs. 'Liakim hugely by that.

The lawyer went into the case with much ease,
   And hugged the belief
   That the cause would be brief,
And settled himself down with hardly a squeeze.
And Bess said, "Keep still, for there's plenty of room,"
And shut down the cover, and left him in gloom.

But scarcely were matters left decently so,
   In walked—not her mother,
   But—worry and bother!—
The mammoth young farmer, whose first name was Joe.
And he gleefully sung, in a heavy bass tone,
   Which came in one note
   From the depths of his throat,
"I'm glad I have come, since I've found you alone.
Let's sit here a while, by this kerosene light,

An' spark it a while now with all of our might."
And Bessie was willing; and so they sat down,
The maiden so fair and the farmer so brown.
They talked of things great, and they talked of things small,

"AND BESS SAID, 'KEEP STILL, FOR THERE'S PLENTY OF ROOM,'
AND SHUT DOWN THE COVER, AND LEFT HIM IN GLOOM."

Which none could condemn,
And which may have pleased them,
But which did not interest the lawyer at all;
And Bessie seemed giving but little concern
To the feelings of him she had shut in the churn.

Till Bessie just artlessly mentioned the man,
And Joe with a will to abuse him began,
And called him full many an ignoble name,
          Appertaining to " Scrubby,"
          And " Shorty," and " Stubby,"
And other descriptions not wide of the same;
And Bessie said naught in the lawyer's behalf,
But seconded Joe, now and then, with a laugh;
And the lawyer said nothing, but winked at his fate,
          And, somewhat abashed,
          And decidedly dashed,
Accepted Joe's motions sans vote or debate.
And several times he, with policy stern,
Repressed a desire to break out of the churn,
Well knowing he thus might get savagely used,
          And if not quite eaten,
          Would likely be beaten,
And probably injured as well as abused.

But now came another quick step at the door,
And Bessie was fearful, the same as before;
And tumbling Joe over a couple of chairs,
          With a general sound
          Of thunder all 'round,
She hurried him up a short pair of back-stairs;
And close in the garret condemned him to wait
Till orders from her, be it early or late.
Then tripping her way down the staircase, she said,
" I'll smuggle them off when the folks get to bed."

It was not her parents; 'twas crafty young Pat,
Returned from his visit; and straightway *he* sat
Beside her, remarking, The chairs were in place,
So he would sit near her, and view her sweet face.
So gayly they talked, as the minutes fast flew,
Discussing such matters as both of them knew,
While often Miss Bessie's sweet laugh answered back,
          For Pat, be it known,
          Had some wit of his own,

And in irony's efforts was sharp as a tack.
And finally Bessie his dancing tongue led,
  By a sly dextrous turn,
  To the man in the churn,
And the farmer, who eagerly listened o'erhead;
Whereat the young Irishman volubly gave

"SEVERAL TIMES HE, WITH POLICY STERN,
REPRESSED A DESIRE TO BREAK OUT OF THE CHURN."

  A short dissertation,
  Whose main information
Was that one was a fool, and the other a knave.

Slim chance there must be for the world e'er to learn
How pleasant this was to the man in the churn;

Though, to borrow a figure lent by his position,
He was doubtless in somewhat a worked-up condition.
It may ne'er be sung, and it may ne'er be said,
How well it was liked by the giant o'erhead.
He lay on a joist—for there wasn't any floor—
   And the joists were so few,
   And so far apart too,
He could not, in comfort, preempt any more;
And he nearly had knocked through the plastering quite,
And challenged young Pat to a fair and square fight;
But he dared not do elsewise than Bessie had said,
For fear, as a lover, he might lose his head.

But now from the meeting the old folks returned,
And sat by the stove as the fire brightly burned;
And Patrick came in from the care of the team;
And since in the house there was overmuch cream,
He thought that the horses their supper might earn,
   And leave him full way
   To plow early next day,
By working that night for a while at the churn.

The old folks consented; and Patrick went out,
Half chuckling, for he had a shrewd Irish doubt,
From various slight sounds he had chanced to discern,
That Bess had a fellow shut up in the churn.

The lawyer, meanwhile, in his hiding-place cooped,
Low-grunted and hitched and contorted and stooped,
But hung to the place like a man in a dream;
And when the young Irishman went for the team,
To stay or to fly, he could hardly tell which;
   But hoping to get
   Neatly out of it yet,
He concluded to hang till the very last hitch.

The churn was one side of the house, recollect,
So rods with the horse-power outside could connect;
And Bess stood so near that she took the lamp's gleam in

"AND THERE HIS PLUMP LIMBS THROUGH THE ORIFICE SWUNG."

While her mother was cheerfully pouring the cream in;
Who, being near-sighted, and minding her cup,
Had no notion of what she was covering up;
But the lawyer, meanwhile, had he dared to have spoke,
Would have owned that he saw the whole cream of the joke.

But just as the voice of young Patrick came strong
And clear through the window, "All ready! go 'long!"
And just as the dasher its motion began,
      Stirred up by its knocks,
      Like a jack-in-the-box
He jumped from his damp, dripping prison—and ran,
And made a frog-leap o'er the stove and a chair,
With some crisp Bible words not intended as prayer.

All over the kitchen he rampaged and tore,
And ran against every thing there but the door;
Tipped over old 'Liakim flat on his back,
And left a long trail of rich cream on his track.
"Ou! ou! 'tis a ghost!" quavered 'Liakim's wife;
"A ghost, if I ever saw one in my life!"
"The devil!" roared 'Liakim, rubbing his shin.
"No! no!" shouted Patrick, who just then came in:
"It's only a lawyer; the devil ne'er runs—
      To bring on him a laugh—
      In the shape of a calf;
It isn't the devil; it's one of his sons!
If so that the spalpeen had words he could utther,
He'd swear he loved Bessie, an' loved no one butther."

Now Joe lay full length on the scantling o'erhead,
      And tried to make out
      What it all was about,
By list'ning to all that was done and was said;
But somehow his balance became uncontrolled,
And he on the plastering heavily rolled.
It yielded instanter, came down with a crash,
And fell on the heads of the folks with a smash.
And there his plump limbs through the orifice swung,

And he caught by the arms and disgracefully hung,
His ponderous body, so clumsy and thick,
Wedged into that posture as tight as a brick.
And 'Liakim Smith, by amazement made dumb
                At those legs in the air
                Hanging motionless there,
Concluded that this time the devil had come;
And seizing a chair, he belabored them well,
While the head pronounced words that no printer would spell.

And there let us leave them, 'mid outcry and clatter,
To come to their wits, and then settle the matter;
And take for the moral this inference fair:
If you're courting a girl, court her honest and square.

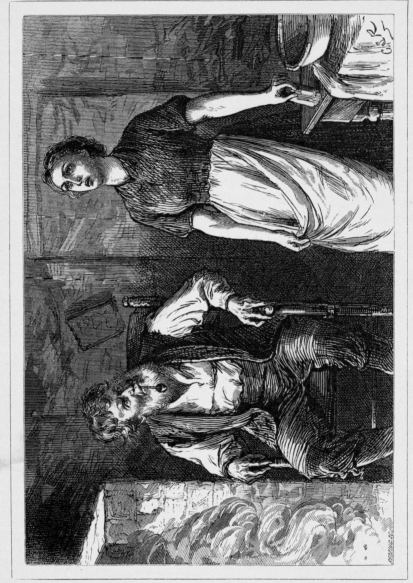

"ALICE, THE COUNTRY MAIDEN, WITH THE SWEET, LOVING FACE,
SUNG THESE WORDS TO AN OLD AIR, WITH AN UNSTUDIED GRACE."

THE SONG OF HOME.

"Sing me a song, my Alice, and let it be your choice,
So as you pipe out plainly, and give me the sweet o' your voice;
An' it be not new-fashioned: the new-made tunes be cold,
An' never awake my fancy like them that's good an' old.
Fie on your high-toned gimcracks, with rests an' beats an' points,
Shaking with trills an' quavers—creakin' in twenty joints!
Sing me the good old tunes, girl, that roll right off the tongue,
Such as your mother gave me when she an' I was young."

So said the Farmer Thompson, smoking his pipe of clay,
Close by his glowing fire-place, at close of a winter day.
He was a lusty fellow, with grizzled beard unshorn,
Hair half combed and flowing, clothing overworn;
Boots of mammoth pattern, with many a patch and rent;
Hands as hard as leather, body with labor bent;
Face of resolution, and lines of pain and care,
Such as the slow world's vanguards are ever doomed to bear;
While from his eyes the yearnings of unemployed desire
Gleamed like the fitful embers of a half-smothered fire.

Alice, the country maiden, with the sweet, loving face,
Sung these words to an old air, with an unstudied grace:

"There's nothing like an old tune, when friends are far apart,
To 'mind them of each other, and draw them heart to heart.
New strains across our senses on magic wings may fly,
But there's nothing like an old tune to make the heart beat high.

"The scenes we have so oft recalled when once again we view,
Have lost the smile they used to wear, and seem to us untrue;
We gaze upon their faded charms with disappointed eye;
And there's nothing like an old tune to make the heart beat high.

5

" We clasp the hands of former friends—we feel again their kiss—
But something that we loved in them, in sorrow now we miss;
For women fade and men grow cold as years go hurrying by;
And there's nothing like an old tune to make the heart beat high.

"The forest where we used to roam, we find it swept away;
The cottage where we lived and loved, it moulders to decay;
And all that feeds our hungry hearts may wither, fade, and die;
There's nothing like an old tune to make the heart beat high."

"That was well sung, my Alice," the farmer proudly said,
When the last strain was finished and the last word had fled;
"That is as true as Gospel; and since you've sung so well,
I'll give you a bit of a story you've never heard me tell.

" When the cry o' the axes first through these parts was heard,
I was young and happy, and chipper as a bird;
Fast as a flock o' pigeons the days appeared to fly,
With no one 'round for a six mile except your mother an' I.
Now we are rich, an' no one except the Lord to thank;
Acres of land all 'round us, money in the bank;
But happiness don't stick by me, an' sunshine ain't so true
As when I was five-an'-twenty, with twice enough to do.

" As for the way your mother an' I made livin' go,
Just some time you ask her—of course she ought to know.
When she comes back in the morning from nursing Rogers' wife,
She'll own she was happy in them days as ever in her life.
For I was sweet on your mother;—why should not I be?
She was the gal I had fought for—she was the world to me;
And since we'd no relations, it never did occur
To me that I was a cent less than all the world to her.

"But it is often doubtful which way a tree may fall;
When you are tol'ble certain, you are not sure at all.
When you are overconscious of travelin' right—that day
Look for a warnin' guide-post that points the other way.
For when you are feeling the safest, it very oft falls out
You rush head-foremost into a big bull-thistle o' doubt.

" 'Twas in the fall o' '50 that I set out, one day,
To hunt for deer an' turkey, or what come in my way;

And wanderin' through the forest, my home I did not seek
Until I was gone from the cabin the better part of a week.

" As Saturday's sun was creeping its western ladder down,
I stopped for a bit of supper at the house of Neighbor Brown.
He was no less my neighbor that he lived ten miles away ;
For neighborhoods then was different from what they are to-day.

" Now Mrs. Brown was clever—a good, well-meaning soul—
And brought to time exactly things under her control.
By very few misgoings were her perfections marred.
She meant well, with one trouble—she meant it 'most too hard.

" Now when I had passed the time o' day, and laughed at Brown's last
    jokes,
Nat'rally I asked 'em if they had seen my folks.
Whereat she shrugged her shoulders quite dangerously-wise,
And looked as if a jury was sittin' in her eyes ;
And after a prudent silence I thought would never end,
Asked if my wife had a brother, or cousin, or other friend ;
For some one, passing my cabin, she'd heard, had lately found
Rather a sleek an' han'some young fellow hanging round ;
Of course it was a brother, or somethin' of that sort?
I told her 'twas a brother, and cut my supper short.

" Which same was wrong, as viewed through a strictly moral eye ;
But who, to shield his wife's name, wouldn't sometime tell a lie ?
'Twas nothing but a lie, girl, and for a lie 'twas meant :
If brothers sold at a million, she couldn't ha' raised a cent.

" Home I trudged in a hurry—who could that fellow be ?
Home I trudged in a hurry, bound that I would see ;
And when I reached my cabin I thought 'twas only fair
To peep in at the window an' find out what was there.

" A nice, good-fashioned fellow as any in the land
Sat by my wife quite closely, a-holdin' of her hand,
An' whispering something into her willin'-listenin' ear,
Which I should judge by her actions she rather liked to hear.

"Now seeing such singular doin's before my very eyes,
The Devil he came upon me, and took me by surprise;
He put his hand on my mouth, girl, and never a word I said,
But raised my gun an' aimed it straight at the stranger's head.

"Lightly I touched the trigger; I drew a good long breath—
My heart was full o' Satan, my aim was full o' death;
But at that very instant they broke out, clear an' strong,
A-singing, both together, a good old-fashioned song.

"That simple little song, girl, still in my ears does ring;
'Twas one I had coaxed your mother while courting her to sing;
Never a word I remember how any verses goes,
But this is a little ditty that every body knows:
How though about a palace you might forever hang,
You'll never feel so happy as in your own shebang.

"It woke the recollections of happy days an' years—
I slowly dropped my rifle, an' melted into tears.
    *   *   *   *   *   *   *

"It was a neighbor's daughter, made on the tomboy plan,
Who, keeping my wife company, had dressed like a spruce young man.
An' full of new-born praises to Him where they belong,
I thanked the Lord for makin' the man who made that good old song."

PAUL'S RUN OFF WITH THE SHOW.

JANE, 'tis so—it is so!
How *can* I—his mother—bear it?
Paul's run off with the show!

Put all his things in the garret—
All o' his working gear;
He's never a-going to wear it,
Never again coming here.
If he gets sick, deaf, or blind,
If he falls and breaks his leg,
He can borrow an organ an' grind,
He can hobble about and beg.
Let him run—good luck behind him!
I wonder which way they went?
I suppose I might follow an' find him.—
But no! let him keep to his bent!
I'm never a-going to go
For a boy that runs off with the show!

Lay his books up in the chamber;
He never will want them now;
Never *did* want them much.
He al'ays could run and clamber,
Make somersets on the mow,
Hand-springs, cart-wheels, an' such,
And other profitless turning;
But when it came to learning,
He would always shirk somehow.

I was trimming him out for a preacher,
When he got over being wild

(He was always a sturdy creature—
A sinfully thrifty child);
A Cartwright preacher, perhaps,
As could eat strong boiled dinners,
Talk straight to saucy chaps,
And knock down fightin' sinners.
I told him of all Heaven's mercies,
Raked his sins o'er and o'er,
Made him learn Scripture verses,
Half a thousand or more;
I sung the hymn-book through him,
I whipped the Bible into him,
In grace to make him grow:
What did such training call for?
What did I name him Paul for?—
To have him run off with a show?

All o' the wicked things
That are found in circus rings,
I taught him to abhor 'em;
But he always was crazy for 'em.
I know what such follies be;
For once in my life—woe's me—
Let's see—
'Twas the fall before Paul was born—
I myself was crazy for shows.
How it happened, Goodness knows;
But howe'er it did befall—
Whate'er may ha' been the reason—
For once I went to all
The circuses of the season.
I watched 'em, high an' low,
Painfully try to be jolly;
I laughed at the tricks o' the clown:
I went and saw their folly,
In order to preach it down:
Little enough did I know
That Paul would run off with a show!

What 'll they do with the boy?
They'll stand him upon a horse,
To his exceeding joy,
To teach him to ride, of course.
Sakes! he can do that now!

"MY BOY! COME IN! COME IN!"

He can whip old Jim to a jump,
And ride upon him standing,
And never get a thump—
Never a bit of harm.
He has trained all the beasts on the farm,

From the ducks to the brindle cow,
To follow his commanding.
Sakes! that it should be so!
Him's I've brought up i' the bosom
Of church, and all things good:
All my pains—I shall lose 'em—
Might have known that I would.
I had hopes beyond my countin',
I had faith as big as a mountain;
But somehow I knew all the while
He'd turn out in some such style—
Always had that fear.

Well, he's never comin' back here.
If he comes to any harm,
If he falls an' sprains his arm,
If he slips and breaks his leg,
He can hobble about an' beg.
He can— Who is that boy out there, Jane,
Skulkin' 'long by the railroad track,
Head an' feet all bare, Jane,
One eye dressed in black?

My boy! Come in! come in!
Come in! come in! come in!
Come in—you sha'n't be hurt.
Come in—you shall rest—you shall rest.
Why, you're all over blood an' dirt!
Did they hurt you?—well, well, it's too bad.
So you thought the old home the best?
You won't run off ag'in?
Well, come in, come in, poor lad;
Come in—come in—come in!

THE KEY TO THOMAS' HEART.

RIDE with me, Uncle Nathan?   *   *
               I don't care an' I do.
My poor old heart's in a hurry; I'm anxious to get through.
My soul outwalks my body; my legs are far from strong;
An' it's mighty kind o' you, doctor, to help the old man along.

I'm some'at full o' hustle; there's business to be done.
I've just been out to the village to see my youngest son.
You used to know him, doctor, ere he his age did get,
An' if I ain't mistaken, you sometimes see him yet.

We took him through his boyhood, with never a ground for fears;
But somehow he stumbled over his early manhood's years.
The landmarks that we showed him, he seems to wander from,
Though in his heart there was never a better boy than Tom.

He was quick o' mind an' body in all he done an' said;
But all the gold he reached for, it seemed to turn to lead.
The devil of grog it caught him, an' held him, though the while
He has never grudged his parents a pleasant word an' smile.

The devil of grog it caught him, an' then he turned an' said,
By that which fed from off him, he henceforth would be fed;
An' that which lived upon him, should give him a livin' o'er;
An' so he keeps that groggery that's next to Wilson's store.

But howsoe'er he's wandered, I've al'ays so far heard
That he had a sense of honor, an' never broke his word;
An' his mother, from the good Lord, she says, has understood
That, if he agrees to be sober, he'll keep the promise good.

An' so when just this mornin' these poor old eyes o' mine
Saw all the women round him, a-coaxin' him to sign,
An' when the Widow Adams let fly a homespun prayer,
An' he looked kind o' wild like, an' started unaware,

An' glanced at her an instant, an' then at his kegs o' rum,
I somehow knew in a minute the turnin'-point had come;

"THE MOTHER, WHO CARRIES THE KEY TO THOMAS' HEART."

An' he would be as good a man as ever yet there's been,
Or else let go forever, an' sink in the sea of sin.

An' I knew, whatever efforts might carry him or fail,
There was only one could help God to turn the waverin' scale;
An' I skulked away in a hurry—I was bound to do my part—
To get the mother, who carries the key to Thomas' heart.

She's gettin' old an' feeble, an' childish in her talk;
An' we've no horse an' buggy, an' she will have to walk;
But she would be fast to come, sir, the gracious chance to seize,
If she had to crawl to Thomas upon her hands an' knees.

   *   *   *   *   *   *   *

Crawl?—walk? No, not if I know it! So set your mind at rest.
Why, hang it! I'm Tom's customer, and said to be his best!
But if this blooded horse here will show his usual power,
Poor Tom shall see his mother in less than half an hour.

THE DOCTOR'S STORY.

I.

Good folks ever will have their way—
Good folks ever for it must pay.

But we, who are here and everywhere,
The burden of their faults must bear.

We must shoulder others' shame—
Fight their follies, and take their blame;

Purge the body, and humor the mind;
Doctor the eyes when the soul is blind;

Build the column of health erect
On the quicksands of neglect:

Always shouldering others' shame—
Bearing their faults and taking the blame!

II.

Deacon Rogers, he came to me;
"Wife is agoin' to die," said he.

"Doctors great, an' doctors small,
Haven't improved her any at all.

"Physic and blister, powders and pills,
And nothing sure but the doctors' bills!

"Twenty women, with remedies new,
Bother my wife the whole day through.

"Sweet as honey, or bitter as gall—
Poor old woman, she takes 'em all.

"Sour or sweet, whatever they choose;
Poor old woman, she daren't refuse.

"So she pleases whoe'er may call,
An' Death is suited the best of all.

"Physic and blister, powder an' pill—
Bound to conquer, and sure to kill!"

III.

Mrs. Rogers lay in her bed,
Bandaged and blistered from foot to head.

Blistered and bandaged from head to toe,
Mrs. Rogers was very low.

Bottle and saucer, spoon and cup,
On the table stood bravely up;

Physics of high and low degree;
Calomel, catnip, boneset tea;

Every thing a body could bear,
Excepting light and water and air.

IV.

I opened the blinds; the day was bright,
And God gave Mrs. Rogers some light.

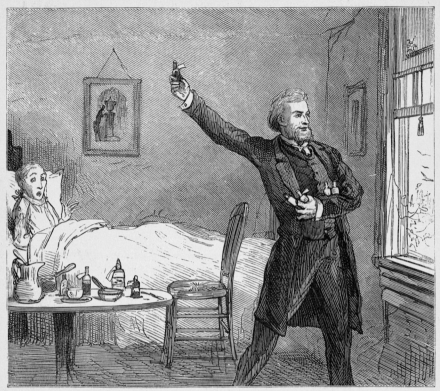

"I THREW THEM AS FAR AS I COULD THROW."

I opened the window; the day was fair,
And God gave Mrs. Rogers some air.

Bottles and blisters, powders and pills,
Catnip, boneset, sirups, and squills;

Drugs and medicines, high and low,
I threw them as far as I could throw.

"What are you doing?" my patient cried;
"Frightening Death," I coolly replied.

"You are crazy!" a visitor said:
I flung a bottle at his head.

V.

Deacon Rogers he came to me;
"Wife is a-gettin' her health," said he.

"I really think she will worry through;
She scolds me just as she used to do.

"All the people have poohed an' slurred—
All the neighbors have had their word;

"'Twere better to perish, some of 'em say,
Than be cured in such an irregular way."

VI.

"Your wife," said I, "had God's good care,
And His remedies, light and water and air.

"All of the doctors, beyond a doubt,
Couldn't have cured Mrs. Rogers without."

VII.

The deacon smiled and bowed his head;
"Then your bill is nothing," he said.

"God's be the glory, as you say!
God bless you, doctor! good-day! good-day!"

VIII.

If ever I doctor that woman again,
I'll give her medicine made by men.

THE CHRISTMAS BABY.

"Tha'rt welcome, little bonny brid,
But shouldn't ha' come just when tha' did:
Teimes are bad."
English Ballad.

Hoot! ye little rascal! ye come it on me this way,
Crowdin' yerself amongst us this blusterin' winter's day,
Knowin' that we already have three of ye, an' seven,
An' tryin' to make yerself out a Christmas present o' Heaven?

Ten of ye have we now, Sir, for this world to abuse;
An' Bobbie he have no waistcoat, an' Nellie she have no shoes,
An' Sammie he have no shirt, Sir (I tell it to his shame),
An' the one that was just before ye we ain't had time to name!

An' all o' the banks be smashin', an' on us poor folk fall;
An' Boss he whittles the wages when work's to be had at all;

An' Tom he have cut his foot off, an' lies in a woful plight,
An' all of us wonders at mornin' as what we shall eat at night;

An' but for your father an' Sandy a-findin' somewhat to do,
An' but for the preacher's woman, who often helps us through,
An' but for your poor dear mother a-doin' twice her part,
Ye'd 'a seen us all in heaven afore *ye* was ready to start!

An' now *ye* have come, ye rascal! so healthy an' fat an' sound,
A-weighin', I'll wager a dollar, the full of a dozen pound!
With yer mother's eyes a flashin', yer father's flesh an' build,
An' a good big mouth an' stomach all ready for to be filled!

No, no! don't cry, my baby! hush up, my pretty one!
Don't get my chaff in yer eye, boy—I only was just in fun.
Ye'll like us when ye know us, although we're cur'us folks;
But we don't get much victual, an' half our livin' is jokes!

Why, boy, did ye take me in earnest? come, sit upon my knee;
I'll tell ye a secret, youngster, I'll name ye after me.
Ye shall have all yer brothers an' sisters with ye to play,
An' ye shall have yer carriage, an' ride out every day!

Why, boy, do ye think ye'll suffer? I'm gettin' a trifle old,
But it 'll be many years yet before I lose my hold;
An' if I should fall on the road, boy, still, them's yer brothers, there,
An' not a rogue of 'em ever would see ye harmed a hair!

Say! when ye come from heaven, my little namesake dear,
Did ye see, 'mongst the little girls there, a face like this one here?
That was yer little sister—she died a year ago,
An' all of us cried like babies when they laid her under the snow!

Hang it! if all the rich men I ever see or knew
Came here with all their traps, boy, an' offered 'em for you,
I'd show 'em to the door, Sir, so quick they'd think it odd,
Before I'd sell to another my Christmas gift from God!

OTHER POEMS.

OTHER POEMS.

―――⊰⊙⊱⊰⊙⊱―――

COVER THEM OVER.

COVER them over with beautiful flowers;
Deck them with garlands, those brothers of ours;
Lying so silent, by night and by day,
Sleeping the years of their manhood away:
Years they had marked for the joys of the brave;
Years they must waste in the sloth of the grave.
All the bright laurels they fought to make bloom
Fell to the earth when they went to the tomb.
Give them the meed they have won in the past;
Give them the honors their merits forecast;
Give them the chaplets they won in the strife;
Give them the laurels they lost with their life.
Cover them over—yes, cover them over—
Parent, and husband, and brother, and lover:
Crown in your heart these dead heroes of ours,
And cover them over with beautiful flowers.

Cover the faces that motionless lie,
Shut from the blue of the glorious sky:
Faces once lit with the smiles of the gay—
Faces now marred by the frown of decay.
Eyes that beamed friendship and love to your own;
Lips that sweet thoughts of affection made known;
Brows you have soothed in the day of distress;
Cheeks you have flushed by the tender caress.

Faces that brightened at War's stirring cry;
Faces that streamed when they bade you good-by;
Faces that glowed in the battle's red flame,
Paling for naught, till the Death Angel came.
Cover them over—yes, cover them over—
Parent, and husband, and brother, and lover:
Kiss in your hearts these dead heroes of ours,
And cover them over with beautiful flowers.

Cover the hands that are resting, half-tried,
Crossed on the bosom, or low by the side:
Hands to you, mother, in infancy thrown;
Hands that you, father, close hid in your own;
Hands where you, sister, when tried and dismayed,
Hung for protection and counsel and aid;
Hands that you, brother, for faithfulness knew;
Hands that you, wife, wrung in bitter adieu.
Bravely the cross of their country they bore;
Words of devotion they wrote with their gore;
Grandly they grasped for a garland of light,
Catching the mantle of death-darkened night.
Cover them over—yes, cover them over—
Parent, and husband, and brother, and lover:
Clasp in your hearts these dead heroes of ours,
And cover them over with beautiful flowers.

Cover the feet that, all weary and torn,
Hither by comrades were tenderly borne:
Feet that have trodden, through love-lighted ways,
Near to your own, in the old happy days;
Feet that have pressed, in Life's opening morn,
Roses of pleasure, and Death's poisoned thorn.
Swiftly they rushed to the help of the right,
Firmly they stood in the shock of the fight.
Ne'er shall the enemy's hurrying tramp
Summon them forth from their death-guarded camp;
Ne'er, till Eternity's bugle shall sound,
Will they come out from their couch in the ground.

Cover them over—yes, cover them over—
Parent, and husband, and brother, and lover:
Rough were the paths of those heroes of ours—
Now cover them over with beautiful flowers.

Cover the hearts that have beaten so high,
Beaten with hopes that were born but to die;
Hearts that have burned in the heat of the fray,
Hearts that have yearned for the homes far away;
Hearts that beat high in the charge's loud tramp,
Hearts that low fell in the prison's foul damp.
Once they were swelling with courage and will,
Now they are lying all pulseless and still;
Once they were glowing with friendship and love,
Now the great souls have gone soaring above.
Bravely their blood to the nation they gave,
Then in her bosom they found them a grave.
Cover them over—yes, cover them over—
Parent, and husband, and brother, and lover:
Press to your hearts these dead heroes of ours,
And cover them over with beautiful flowers.

One there is, sleeping in yonder low tomb,
Worthy the brightest of flow'rets that bloom.
Weakness of womanhood's life was her part;
Tenderly strong was her generous heart.
Bravely she stood by the sufferer's side,
Checking the pain and the life-bearing tide;
Fighting the swift-sweeping phantom of Death,
Easing the dying man's fluttering breath;
Then, when the strife that had nerved her was o'er,
Calmly she went to where wars are no more.
Voices have blessed her now silent and dumb;
Voices will bless her in long years to come.
Cover her over—yes, cover her over—
Blessings, like angels, around her shall hover;
Cherish the name of that sister of ours,
And cover her over with beautiful flowers.

"THEY WHO IN MOUNTAIN AND HILL-SIDE AND DELL
REST WHERE THEY WEARIED, AND LIE WHERE THEY FELL."

Cover the thousands who sleep far away—
Sleep where their friends can not find them to-day;
They who in mountain and hill-side and dell
Rest where they wearied, and lie where they fell.
Softly the grass-blade creeps round their repose;
Sweetly above them the wild flow'ret blows;
Zephyrs of freedom fly gently o'erhead,
Whispering names for the patriot dead.
So in our minds we will name them once more,
So in our hearts we will cover them o'er;

Roses and lilies and violets blue
Bloom in our souls for the brave and the true.
Cover them over—yes, cover them over—
Parent, and husband, and brother, and lover:
Think of those far-away heroes of ours,
And cover them over with beautiful flowers.

When the long years have crept slowly away,
E'en to the dawn of Earth's funeral day;
When, at the Archangel's trumpet and tread,
Rise up the faces and forms of the dead;
When the great world its last judgment awaits;
When the blue sky shall swing open its gates,
And our long columns march silently through,
Past the Great Captain, for final review;
Then for the blood that has flown for the right,
Crowns shall be given, untarnished and bright;
Then the glad ear of each war-martyred son
Proudly shall hear the good judgment, "Well done."
Blessings for garlands shall cover them over—
Parent, and husband, and brother, and lover:
God will reward those dead heroes of ours,
And cover them over with beautiful flowers.

RIFTS IN THE CLOUD.

[Graduating Poem, June 17, 1869.]

Life is a cloud—e'en take it as you may;
Illumine it with Pleasure's transient ray;
Brighten its edge with Virtue; let each fold
E'en by the touch of God be flecked with gold,
While angel-wings may kindly hover near,
And angel-voices murmur words of cheer,
Still, life's a cloud, forever hanging nigh,
    Forever o'er our winding pathways spread,
Ready to blacken on some saddened eye,
    And hurl its bolts on some defenseless head.

Yes, there are lives that seem to know no ill;
Paths that seem straight, with naught of thorn or hill.
The bright and glorious sun, each welcome day,
Flashes upon the flowers that deck their way,
And the soft zephyr sings a lullaby,
'Mid rustling trees, to please the ear and eye;
And all the darling child of fortune needs,
And all his dull, half-slumbering caution heeds,
While fairy eyes their watch above him keep,
Is breath to live and weariness to sleep.
But life's a cloud! and soon the smiling sky
    May wear the unwelcome semblance of a frown,
And the fierce tempest, madly rushing by,
    May raise its dripping wings, and strike him down!

When helpless infancy, for love or rest,
Lies nestling to a mother's yearning breast,
While she, enamored of its ways and wiles
As mothers only are, looks down and smiles,

And spies a thousand unsuspected charms
In the sweet babe she presses in her arms,
While he, the love-light kindled in his eyes,
Sends to her own, electrical replies,
A ray of sunshine comes for each caress,
From out the clear blue sky of happiness.
But life's a cloud! and soon the smiling face
   The frowns and tears of childish grief may know,
And the love-language of the heart give place
   To the wild clamor of a baby's woe.

The days of youth are joyful in their way;
Bare feet tread lightly, and their steps are gay.
Parental kindness grades the early path,
And shields it from the storm-king's dreaded wrath.
But there are thorns that prick the infant flesh,
And bid the youthful eyes to flow afresh,
Thorns that maturer nerves would never feel,
With wounds that bleed not less, that soon they heal.
When we look back upon our childhood days,
Look down the long and sweetly verdant ways
Wherein we gayly passed the shining hours,
We see the beauty of its blooming flowers,
We breathe its fresh and fragrant air once more,
And, counting all its many pleasures o'er,
And giving them their natural place of chief,
Forget our disappointments and our grief.
Sorrows that now were light, then weighed us down,
And claimed our tears for every surly frown.
For life's a cloud, e'en take it as we will,
   The changing wind ne'er banishes or lifts;
The pangs of grief but make it darker still,
   And happiness is nothing but its rifts.

There is a joy in sturdy manhood still;
Bravery is joy; and he who says, I WILL,
And turns, with swelling heart, and dares the fates,
While firm resolve upon his purpose waits,

Is happier for the deed; and he whose share
Is honest toil, pits that against dull care.
And yet, in spite of labor, faith, or prayer,
    Dark clouds and fearful o'er our paths are driven;
They take the shape of monsters in the air,
    And almost shut our eager gaze from heaven!

Disease is there, with slimy, loathsome touch,
With hollow, blood-shot eyes and eager clutch,
Longing to strike us down with pangs of pain,
And bind us there, with weakness' galling chain.
Ruin is there, with cunning ambush laid,
Waiting some panic in the ranks of trade,
Some profitless endeavor, or some trust
By recreant knave abused, to snatch the crust
From out the mouths of them we love the best,
And bring gaunt hunger, an unwelcome guest.
Disgrace is there, of honest look bereft,
Truth in his right hand, falsehood in his left,
Pride in his mouth, the devil in his eye,
His garment truth, his cold black heart a lie,
Forging the bolts to blast some honored name;
    Longing to see some victim wronged or wrong;
To see him step into the pool of shame,
    Or soiled by loved ones that to him belong.

A dark cloud hovers over every zone—
The cloud of ignorance. The great unknown,
Defying comprehension, still hangs low
Above our feeble minds. When we who now
Have stumbled 'neath the ever-varying load
That marks the weary student's royal road,
Have hurried over verbs in headlong haste,
And various thorny paths of language traced;
Have run our muddled heads, with rueful sigh,
'Gainst figures truthful, that yet seemed to lie;
Have peeped into the Sciences, and learned
How much we do not know; have bravely turned

Our guns of eloquence on forest trees,
And preached grave doctrines to the wayward breeze;
When we have done all this, the foggy cloud,
With scarce a rift, is still above us bowed;
And we are children, on some garden's verge,
   Groping for flowers the opposing wall beneath,
Who, flushed and breathless, may at last emerge,
   With a few scanty blossoms for a wreath.

But never was a cloud so thick and black,
But it might some time break, and on its track
The glorious sun come streaming. Never, too,
So but its threads might bleach to lighter hue,
Was sorrow's mantle of so deep a dye.
And he who, peering at the troubled sky,
Looks past the clouds, or looks the cloud-rifts through,
   Or, finding none, remembers their great worth,
And strikes them for himself, is that man who
   Shows the completest wisdom of this earth.

When one stands forth in Reason's glorious light,
Stands in his own proud consciousness of right,
Laments his faults, his virtues does not boast,
Studies all creatures—and himself the most—
Knowing the way wherewith his faults to meet,
Or, vanquished by them, owning his defeat,
He pays the penalty as should a man,
And pitches battle with the foe again;
When, giving all their proper due and heed,
He yet has power, when such shall be the need,
To go his way, unshackled, true, and free,
And bid the world go hanged, if needs must be,
He strikes a rift for his unfearing eye
Through the black cloud of low servility:
A cloud that's decked the Orient all these years;
'Neath whose low-bending folds, 'mid groans and tears,
Priestcraft has heaped its huge, ill-gotten gains,
And tyrants forged their bloody, clanking chains;

A cloud, that when the *Mayflower's* precious cup
The misty, treacherous deep held proudly up,
By waves that leaped and dashed each other o'er,
But onward still the ark of Freedom bore,
Some fair and peaceful Ararat to find,
Plumed its black wings, and swept not far behind.
To-day it lowers o'er this great, free land—
    O'er farms and workshops, offices and spires—
Its baleful shadow casts on every hand,
    And darkens Church and State and household fires.

It is a thing to pity and to blame,
A useless, vile, humiliating shame,
A silent slander on the Heaven-born soul,
Decked with the signet of its own control,
A flaw upon the image of our God,
When men, obedient to some Mogul's nod—
When men, the sockets of whose addled brains
Are blessed with some illuminate remains
Wherefrom the glim of reason still is shed,
Blow out the light, and send their wits to bed;
And, taking as their sole dictator, then,
Some little, thundering god of speech or pen,
Aping submissively the smile or frown
Of some great brazen face that beats them down,
Or silenced by some lubricated tongue,
Covered with borrowed words and neatly hung—
They yield their judgments up to others' wills,
And take grave creeds like sugar-coated pills;
And, with their weakness tacitly confessed,
Like the unfeathered fledgelings of a nest,
When the old bird comes home with worms and flies—
    With half a smile and half a knowing frown,
They open wide their mouths, and shut their eyes,
    And seem to murmur softly, *"Drop it down."*

He who will creep about some great man's feet,
The honeyed fragrance of his breath to meet,

Or follow him about, with crafty plan,
And cringe for smiles and favors, is no man.
A fraction of a man, and all his own,
Although his numerator be but one,
With unity divided up so fine
That thousands range themselves beneath the line—
Ay, one so insignificantly small
That quick accountants count him not at all—
Is better far, and vastly nobler, too,
    Than some great swelling cipher among men,
Naught of itself, and nothing else to do
    Except to help some little one count ten!

Let us e'en strike, with courage true endowed,
Straight at the centre of this murky cloud,
And sweep its worthless vapor from the earth.
Take sense for coin; opinions at their worth;
Conviction at its cost; dictation, when
Our minds and souls are bankrupt—hardly then!
When Freedom's sons and daughters will do this,
Our land will know a day of happiness,
Fit for such joy as never yet was seen,
E'en when Emancipation tried her keen
Bright blade upon the galling chains of steel,
And stamped the action with the nation's seal.
E'en when the cable its initial spark
Brought flashing through the ocean's deep and dark;
E'en when was fixed, with far-resounding strokes,
    With song, and praise, and thankfulness, and mirth,
The golden fastening of the chain that yokes
    The two great restless oceans of the earth!

But over all, and round about us spread,
Hangs the black cloud of Death: a thunder-head,
Yet ominously silent; moving on,
    While from its threatening folds, so deep and dark,
The forkèd lightning, ever and anon,
    Shoots for some life, and never fails its mark.

7

There was one classmate is not here to-day;
Many an oak is blasted on its way,
Many a growing hope is overthrown.
What might have been, his early growth had shown;
What was, our love and tears for him may tell;
He lived, he toiled, he faded, and he fell.
When our friend lay within that narrow room
Men call a coffin—in its cheerless gloom
Himself the only tenant, and asleep
In a long slumber, terrible and deep;
When at the open door his pale, sad face
Appeared to us, without a look or trace
Of recognition in its ghastly hue,
Soon to be hid forever from our view;
When, with his sightless eyes to heaven upturned,
Wherefrom his royal soul upon them burned,
He waited for his last rites to be said,
With the pathetic patience of the dead;
When tenderly his manly form we lay
In its last couch, with covering of clay;
Who in that mournful duty had a part,
But felt the cloud of Death upon his heart?
But when we thought how his unfettered soul,
Free from his poor sick body's weak control,
Pluming its wings at the Eternal throne,
   Might take through realms of space its rapid flight,
And find a million joys to us unknown,
   The cloud was rifted by a ray of light.

Old class of '69! together, still,
We've journeyed up the rough and toilsome hill;
Seeking the gems to labor ne'er denied,
Plucking the fruits that deck the mountain-side.
Now, in the glory of this summer day,
We part, and each one goes his different way.
Let each, with hope to fire his yearning soul,
Still hurry onward to the shining goal.
The way at times may dark and weary seem,
No ray of sunshine on our path may beam,

The dark clouds hover o'er us like a pall,
And gloom and sadness seem to compass all;
But still, with honest purpose, toil we on;
   And if our steps be upright, straight, and true,
Far in the east a golden light shall dawn,
   And the bright smile of God come bursting through.

SOME TIME.

O STRONG and terrible Ocean,
O grand and glorious Ocean,
O restless, stormy Ocean, a million fathoms o'er!
When never an eye was near thee to view thy turbulent glory,
When never an ear to hear thee relate thy endless story,

What didst thou then, O Ocean? Didst toss thy foam in air,
With never a bark to fear thee, and never a soul to dare?

"Oh, I was the self-same Ocean,
The same majestic Ocean,
The strong and terrible Ocean, with rock-embattled shore;
I threw my fleecy blanket up over my shoulders bare,
I raised my head in triumph, and tossed my grizzled hair;
For I knew that some time—some time—
White-robed ships would venture from out of the placid bay,
Forth to my heaving bosom, my lawful pride or prey;
I knew that some time—some time—
Lordly men and maidens my servile guests would be,
And hearts of sternest courage would falter and bend to me."

O deep and solemn Forest,
O sadly whispering Forest,
O lonely moaning Forest, that murmureth evermore!
When never a footstep wandered across thy sheltered meadows,
When never a wild bird squandered his music 'mid thy shadows,
What didst thou then, O Forest? Didst robe thyself in green,
And pride thyself in beauty the while to be unseen?
"Oh, I was the self-same Forest,
The same low-whispering Forest,
The softly murmuring Forest, and all of my beauties wore.
I dressed myself in splendor all through the lonely hours;
I twined the vines around me, and covered my lap with flowers;
For I knew that some time—some time—
Birds of beautiful plumage would flit and nestle here;
Songs of marvelous sweetness would charm my listening ear;
I knew that some time—some time—
Lovers would gayly wander 'neath my protecting boughs,
And into the ear of my silence would whisper holy vows."

O fair and beautiful Maiden,
O pure and winsome Maiden,
O grand and peerless Maiden, created to adore!
When no love came to woo thee that won thy own love-treasure,
When never a heart came to thee thy own heart-wealth could measure,
What didst thou then, O Maiden? Didst smile as thou smilest now,
With ne'er the kiss of a lover upon thy snow-white brow?

"Oh, I was the self-same Maiden,
The simple and trusting Maiden,
The happy and careless Maiden, with all of my love in store.
I gayly twined my tresses, and cheerfully went my way;
I took no thought of the morrow, and cared for the cares of the day;
For I knew that some time—some time—
Into the path of my being the Love of my life would glide,
And we by the gates of heaven would wander side by side."

BROTHERS AND FRIENDS.

[Reunion of Alpha Kappa Phi Society, June 16, 1875.]

Would I might utter all my heart can feel!
But there are thoughts weak words will not reveal.
The rarest fruitage is the last to fall;
The strongest language hath no words at all.

When first the uncouth student comes in sight—
A sturdy plant, just struggling toward the light—
Arriving at his future classic home,
He gazes at the high-perched college dome,
Striving, through eyes with a vague yearning dim,
To spy some future glory there for him,
A child in thought, a man in strong desire,
A clod of clay, vexed by a restless fire,

When, with hard hands, and uncongenial locks,
And clothes as speckled as young Jacob's flocks,
Homesick and heart-sick, tired and desolate,
He leans himself 'gainst Learning's iron gate,
While all the future frowns upon his track,
And all the past conspires to pull him back;
When, with tired resolution in his looks,
He bends above the cabalistic books,
And strives, with knitted forehead throbbing hot,
To learn what older students have forgot;
And wonders how the Romans and the Greeks
Could cry aloud and spare their jaws and cheeks;
And wants the Algebraic author put
On an equation, tied there, head and foot,

Which then, with all Reduction's boasted strength,
May be expanded to prodigious length;
When he reflects, with rueful, pain-worn phiz,
What a sad, melancholy dog he is,
And how much less unhappy and forlorn
Are all those students who are not yet born;
When Inexperience like a worm is twined
Around the clumsy fingers of his mind,
And Discipline, a stranger yet unknown,
Struts grandly by and leaves him all alone;
What cheers him better than to feel and see
Some other one as badly off as he?
Or the sincere advice and kindly aid
Of those well worked in Study's curious trade?
What help such solace and improvement lends
As the hand-grasp of Brothers and of Friends?

When, with a wildly ominous halloo,
The frisky Freshman shuffles into view,
And shouts aloud the war-cry of his clan,
And makes friends with the devil like a man;
When, looking upward at the other classes,
He dubs them as three tandem-teams of asses,
And, scarcely knowing what he does it for,
Vows against them unmitigated war,
And aims to show them that though they may tread
In stately, grand procession o'er his head,
The animated pathway that they scorn,
May sometimes bristle with a hidden thorn;
When, with a vigilance that to nothing yields,
He scans the fruitage of the neighboring fields,
And in the solemn night-time doth entwine
Affection's fingers round the melon-vine;
When the tired wagon from its sheltering shed
To strange, uncouth localities is led,
And, with the night for a dissecting-room,
Is analyzed amid the friendly gloom;
When the hushed rooster, cheated of his cry,
From his spoiled perch bids this vain world good-bye;

When, in the chapel, an unwilling guest,
And living sacrifice, a cow doth rest;
When from the tower, the bell's notes, pealing down,
Rouse up the fireman from the sleeping town,
Who, rushing to the scene, with duty fired,
Finds his well-meant assistance unrequired,
And, creeping homeward, steadily doth play
Upon the third commandment all the way;
When are played off, with mirth-directed aims,
At the staid Alma Mater, various games,
As feline juveniles themselves regale
In the lithe folds of the maternal tail,
And when these antics have gone far enough,
Comes from her paw a well-considered cuff,
What more to soothe the chastened spirit tends
Than sympathy from Brothers and from Friends?

When the deep Sophomore has well begun
The study of his merits, one by one,
And found that he, a bright scholastic blade,
Is fearfully and wonderfully made;
Discovers how much greater is his share
Of genius than he was at first aware;
When, with a ken beyond his tender age,
He sweeps o'er History's closely printed page,
Conjecturing how this world so long endured,
With his co-operation unsecured;
When, with his geometrical survey
Trigonometrically brought in play,
He scans two points, with firm, unmoved design
To join them sooner than by one straight line;
When he, with oratoric hand astir,
Rolls back the tide of ages—as it were;
When Cicero he decides for reading fit,
And tolerates happy Horace for his wit;
When he across Zoölogy takes sight,
To see what creatures were created right,
And looks the plants that heaven has fashioned through,
To see if they were rightly finished, too;

When he his aid to any cause can lend,
In readiness, on short notice, to ascend
From any well-worn point, secure and soon,
In his small oratorical balloon,
Expecting, when his high trip's end appears,
Descent upon a parachute of cheers;
When he decides, beneath a load of care,
What whiskered monogram his face shall wear;
When, from his mind's high shoulders cropping out,
Linguistic feathers constantly do sprout,
Which, ere they meet the cool outsider's scoff,
Require a quiet, friendly picking-off;
What better to this operation lends
Than the critiques of Brothers and of Friends?

When the spruce Junior, not disposed to shirk,
Begins to get down fairly to his work,
Strives to run foremost in the college race,
Or at least fill a creditable place;
When he bears, o'er the rough and hard highway,
The heat and burden of the college day,
And hastes—his mental lungs all out of breath—
As if it were a race of life and death;
When with some little doubt his brain is fraught,
That he's not quite so brilliant as he thought,
And he would strengthen his lame talent still,
By wrapping 'round the bandage of his will;
When, undergoing the reaction drear
That follows up the Sophomoric year,
He finds each task much harder than before,
And tarries long at every phrase's door,
And pauses o'er his dull oration's page,
Then tears it into pieces in a rage;
When, had he fifty ink-stands, he could throw
Each at some devil fraught with fancied woe;
And when, perchance, atop of all this gloom,
In his heart's world there's yet sufficient room
For Cupid to come blundering through the dark,
And make his sensibilities a mark,

And, viewing each the other from afar,
Learning and Love frown miserably, and spar;
What for his trouble-phantoms makes amends
Like the support of Brothers and of Friends?

When, with a strengthened soul and chastened brain,
The Senior who has labored not in vain
Looks back upon the four eventful years
Most fruitful that in his past life appears,
When he stands, somewhat shadowed by remorse,
In the bright Indian Summer of the course,
And muses, had each opportunity
Been seized, how smooth his present path might be;
When, having blundered through each college hall,
Bumping his head 'gainst Inexperience' wall,
There burst upon him through the window-panes,
Broad Knowledge' deep ravines and fertile plains;
When, standing at the door, with gaze of doubt,
He draws on his world-wrappings, and looks out
Into the chillness of the winter's day,
And almost wishes that he still might stay,
What nearer to his beating heart extends
Than parting with his Brothers and his Friends?

When he at last has bid the school good-by,
And finds that many matters go awry;
Finds much amid Earth's uncongenial fog,
Not mentioned in the college catalogue;
Finds that The World, in writing his name down,
Forgets, somehow, to add the letters on
Which serve to make his fellow-mortals see
How little rests behind a big degree;
Finds, also, that it is inclined to speak
Elsewise than in the Latin or the Greek;
Finds that the sharp blade of his brightened mind
Gets dulled upon the pachydermal kind;
That The World by Declension understands
The sliding-down of houses, stocks, and lands;

And that Translation means, in this world's bother,
Translation from one pocket to another;
Mistrusts that if The World has, as is sung,
A tail by which, perchance, it may be slung,
The blessed place so many hands infold,
He can not find whereon he may take hold;
Finds that he best makes ground o'er this world's road,
As he his college nonsense doth unload;
What sweeter sound with Life's alarum blends
Than the kind voice of Brothers and of Friends?

*   *   *   *   *   *   *

And so, to-day, we live our old lives o'er—
The Freshman gay, the smiling Sophomore,
The anxious Junior, and the Senior proud,
The care-immersed Alumnus, sober-browed;
To shake once more the quick-responding hand,
To trade in jokes no others understand;
Our fish-lines into Memory's ponds to throw
For stories which were left there long ago
(Which, like most fishy ventures, as is known,
Through many changing years have bred and grown);
To beat the big drum of our vanity,
To clash the cymbals of our boisterous glee;
To bind again the old-time friendships fast,
To fight once more the battles of the past.

Beneath the blue of the clear sunlit sky,
Beneath the storm-cloud, rudely lingering nigh,
From night to night—from changing day to day—
The Alpha Kappa Phi has won its way.
And as the lichen plant, when tempest-torn,
And roughly from its native hill-side borne,
Sucks moisture from the whirlwind's shivering form,
And grows, while yet hurled onward by the storm,
And when at last its voyage well is o'er,
Thrives sweeter, purer, stronger than before,
The Alpha Kappa Phi has ever grown
Stronger for all the struggles it has known;
And, 'mid the smiles and frowns that heaven out-sends,
Our hearts still beat as Brothers and as Friends.

GONE BEFORE.

I.

PULL up the window-lattice, Jane, and raise me in my bed,
  And trim my beard, and brush my hair, and from this covering free
    me,
And brace me back against the wall, and raise my aching head,
  And make me trim, for one I love is coming here to see me;
Or if she do not see me, Jane, 'twill be that her dear eyes
  Are shut as ne'er they shut before, in all of their reposing;
For never yet my lowest word has failed of kind replies,
  And ever still my lightest touch has burst her eyelids' closing;
                    So let her come to me.

They say she's coming in her sleep—a sleep they can not break;
  Ay, let them call, and let them weep, in dull and droning fashion!
Her ear may hear their doleful tones an age and never wake;
  But let me pour into its depth my words of burning passion!
Ay, let my hot and yearning lips, that long have yearned in vain,
  But press her pure and sacred cheek, and wander in her tresses;
And let my tears no more be lost, but on her forehead rain,
  And she will rise and pity me, and soothe me with caresses;
                    So let her come to me.

O silver-crested days agone, that wove us in one heart!
  O golden future years, that urged our hands to clasp in striving!
There is not that in earth or sky can hold us two apart;
  And I of her, and she of me, not long may know depriving!
So bring her here, where I have long in absence pining lain,
  While on my fevered weakness crashed the castles of our building;

And once together, all the woe and weary throbs of pain
   That strove to cloud our happiness shall be its present gilding;
              So let her come to me.

II.

They brought her me—they brought her me—they bore her to my bed;
   And first I marked her coffin's form, and saw its jewels glisten.
I talked to her, I wept to her, but she was cold and dead;
   I prayed to her, and then I knew she was not here to listen.
For Death had wooed and won my love, and carried her away.
   How could she know my trusting heart, and then so sadly grieve
      me!
Her hand was his, her cheek was his, her lips of ashen gray;
   Her heart was never yet for him, however she might leave me;
            Her heart was e'er for me.

O waves that well had sunk my life, sweep back to me again!
   I will not fight your coming now, or flee from your pursuing!
But bear me, beat me, dash me to the land of Death, and then
   I'll find the love Death stole from me, and scorn him with my wooing!
Oh, I will light his gloomy orbs with jealous, mad surprise;
   Oh, I will crush his pride, e'en with the lack of my endeavor;
The while I boldly bear away, from underneath his eyes,
   The soul that God had made for me—to lose no more forever;
           Ay, she will go with me.

Pull down the window-lattice, Jane, and turn me in my bed,
   And not until the set of sun be anxious for my waking;
And ere that hour a robe of light above me shall be spread,
   And darkness here shall show me there the morn that now is breaking.
And in one grave let us be laid—my truant love and me—
   And side by side shall rest the hearts that once were one in beating;
And soon together and for aye our wedded souls shall be,
   And never cloud shall dim again the brightness of our meeting,
          Where now she waits for me.

THE LITTLE SLEEPER.

THERE is mourning in the cottage as the twilight shadows fall,
For a little rose-wood coffin has been brought into the hall,
   And a little pallid sleeper,
   In a slumber colder, deeper
Than the nights of life could give her, in its narrow borders lies,
With the sweet and changeful lustre ever faded from her eyes.

Since the morning of her coming, but a score of suns had set,
And the strangeness of the dawning of her life is with her yet;
   And the dainty lips asunder
   Are a little pressed with wonder,
And her smiling bears the traces of a shadow of surprise,
But the wondering mind that made it looks no more from out her eyes.

'Twas a soul upon a journey, and was lost upon its way;
'Twas a flash of light from heaven on a tiny piece of clay;
   'Twas more timid, and yet bolder,
   It was younger, and yet older,
It was weaker, and yet stronger, than this little human guise,
With the strange unearthly lustre ever faded from its eyes.

They will bury her the morrow; they will mourn her as she died;
I will bury her the morrow, and another by her side;
   For the raven hair, but started,
   Soon a maiden would have parted,
Full of fitful joy and sorrow—gladly gay and sadly wise;
With a dash of worldly mischief in her deep and changeful eyes.

I will bury her the morrow, and another by her side:
It shall be a wife and mother, full of love and care and pride;
   Full of hope, and of misgiving;
   Of the joys and griefs of living;

Of the pains of others' being, and the tears of others' cries;
With the love of God encompassed in her smiling, weeping eyes.

I will bury on the morrow, too, a grandame, wrinkled, old;
One whose pleasures of the present were the joys that had been told;
   I will bury one whose blessing
   Was the transport of caressing
Every joy that she had buried—every lost and broken prize;
With a gleam of heaven-expected, in her dim and longing eyes.

I will joy for her to-morrow, as I see her compassed in,
For the lips now pure and holy might be some time stained with sin;
   And the brow now white and stainless,
   And the heart now light and painless,
Might have throbbed with guilty passion, and with sin-encumbered sighs
Might have surged the sea of brightness in the bright and changeful eyes.

Let them bury her to-morrow—let them treasure her away;
Let the soul go back to heaven, and the body back to clay;
   Let the future grief here hidden,
   Let the happiness forbidden,
Be for evermore forgotten, and be buried as it dies,
And an angel let us see her, with our sad and weeping eyes.

'TIS SNOWING.

FIRST VOICE.

Hurra! 'tis snowing!
On street and house-roof, gently cast,
The falling flakes come thick and fast;
They wheel and curve from giddy height,
And speck the chilly air with white!
Come on, come on, you light-robed storm!
My fire within is blithe and warm,
     And brightly glowing!
My robes are thick, my sledge is gay;
My champing steeds impatient neigh;
My silver-sounding bells are clear,
With music for the muffled ear;
And she within—my queenly bride—
Shall sit right gayly by my side;
     Hurra! 'tis snowing!

SECOND VOICE.

Good God! 'tis snowing!
From out the dull and leaden clouds,
The surly storm impatient crowds;
It beats against my fragile door,
It creeps across my cheerless floor;
And through my pantry, void of fare,
And o'er my hearth, so cold and bare,
     The wind is blowing;
And she who rests her weary head
Upon our hard and scanty bed,
Prays hopefully, but hopeless still,
For bright spring days and whip-poor-will;

8

The damp of death is at her brow,
The frost is at her feet; and now
   'Tis drearily snowing.

FIRST VOICE.

   Hurra! 'tis snowing!
Snow on! ye can not stop our ride,
As o'er the white-paved road we glide:
Past forest trees thick draped with snow,
Past white-thatched houses, quaint and low;
Past rich-stored barn and stately herd,
Past well-filled sleigh and kindly word,
   Right gayly going!
Snow on! for when our ride is o'er,
And once again we reach the door,
Our well-filled larder shall provide,
Our cellar-doors shall open wide;
And while without 'tis cold and drear,
Within, our board shall smile with cheer,
   Although 'tis snowing!

SECOND VOICE.

   Good God! 'tis snowing!
Rough men now bear, with hurried tread,
My pauper wife unto her bed;
And while, all crushed, but unresigned,
I cringe and follow close behind,
And while these scalding, bitter tears—
The first that stain my manhood years—
   Are freely flowing,
Her waiting grave is open wide,
And into it the snow-flakes glide.
A mattress for her couch they wreathe;
And snow above, and snow beneath,
Must be the bed of her who prayed
The sun might shine where she was laid;
   And still 'tis snowing!

THE BURNING OF CHICAGO.

I.

'TWAS night in the beautiful city,
The famous and wonderful city,
The proud. and magnificent city,
The Queen of the North and the West.
The riches of nations were gathered in wondrous and plentiful store;
The swift-speeding bearers of Commerce were waiting on river and shore;
The great staring walls towered skyward, with visage undaunted and bold,
And said, "We are ready, O Winter! come on with your hunger and
    cold!
Sweep down with your storms from the northward! come out from your
    ice-guarded lair!
Our larders have food for a nation! our wardrobes have clothing to spare!
For off from the corn-bladed prairies, and out from the valleys and hills,
The farmer has swept us his harvests, the miller has emptied his mills;
And here, in the lap of our city, the treasures of autumn shall rest,
In golden-crowned, glorious Chicago, the Queen of the North and the
    West!"

II.

'Twas night in the church-guarded city,
The temple and altar-decked city,
The turreted, spire-adorned city,
The Queen of the North and the West.
And out from the beautiful temples that wealth in its fullness had made,
And out from the haunts that were humble, where Poverty peacefully
    prayed,
Where praises and thanks had been offered to Him where they rightly
    belonged,
In peacefulness quietly homeward the worshiping multitude thronged.

The Pharisee, laden with riches and jewelry, costly and rare,
Who proudly deigned thanks to Jehovah he was not as other men are;
The penitent, crushed in his weakness, and laden with pain and with sin;
The outcast who yearningly waited to hear the glad bidding, "Come in;"
And thus went they quietly homeward, with sins and omissions confessed,
In spire-adorned, templed Chicago, the Queen of the North and the West.

III.

'Twas night in the sin-burdened city,
The turbulent, vice-laden city,
The sin-compassed, rogue-haunted city,
Though Queen of the North and the West.
And low in their caves of pollution great beasts of humanity growled;
And over his money-strewn table the gambler bent fiercely, and scowled;
And men with no seeming of manhood, with countenance flaming and
fell,
Drank deep from the fire-laden fountains that spring from the rivers of
hell;
And men with no seeming of manhood, who dreaded the coming of day,
Prowled, cat-like, for blood-purchased plunder from men who were bet-
ter than they;
And men with no seeming of manhood, whose dearest-craved glory was
shame,
Whose joys were the sorrows of others, whose harvests were acres of
flame,
Slunk, whispering and low, in their corners, with bowie and pistol tight-
pressed,
In rogue-haunted, sin-cursed Chicago, though Queen of the North and
the West.

IV.

'Twas night in the elegant city,
The rich and voluptuous city,
The beauty-thronged, mansion-decked city,
Gay Queen of the North and the West.

And childhood was placidly resting in slumber untroubled and deep;
And softly the mother was fondling her innocent baby to sleep;
And maidens were dreaming of pleasures and triumphs the future should show,
And scanning the brightness and glory of joys they were never to know;
And firesides were cheerful and happy, and Comfort smiled sweetly around;
But grim Desolation and Ruin looked into the window and frowned.
And pitying angels looked downward, and gazed on their loved ones below,
And longed to reach forth a deliverance, and yearned to beat backward the foe;
But Pleasure and Comfort were reigning, nor danger was spoken or guessed,
In beautiful, golden Chicago, gay Queen of the North and the West.

v.

Then up in the streets of the city,
The careless and negligent city,
The soon to be sacrificed city,
Doomed Queen of the North and the West,
Crept, softly and slyly, so tiny it hardly was worthy the name,
Crept, slowly and soft through the rubbish, a radiant serpent of flame.
The South-wind and West-wind came shrieking, "Rouse up in your strength and your ire!
For many a year they have chained you, and crushed you, O demon of fire!
For many a year they have bound you, and made you their servant and slave!
Now, rouse you, and dig for this city a fiery and desolate grave!
Freight heavy with grief and with wailing her world-scattered pride and renown!
Charge straight on her mansions of splendor, and battle her battlements down!
And we, the strong South-wind and West-wind, with thrice-doubled fury possessed,
Will sweep with you over this city, this Queen of the North and the West!"

VI.

Then straight at the great, quiet city,
The strong and o'erconfident city,
The well-nigh invincible city,
Doomed Queen of the North and the West.
The Fire-devil rallied his legions, and speeded them forth on the wind,
With tinder and treasures before him, with ruins and tempests behind.
The tenement crushed 'neath his footstep, the mansion oped wide at his
  knock;
And walls that had frowned him defiance, they trembled and fell with
  a shock;
And down on the hot, smoking house-tops came raining a deluge of fire;
And serpents of flame writhed and clambered, and twisted on steeple and
  spire;
And beautiful, glorious Chicago, the city of riches and fame,
Was swept by a storm of destruction, was flooded by billows of flame.
The Fire-king loomed high in his glory, with crimson and flame-stream-
  ing crest,
And grinned his fierce scorn on Chicago, doomed Queen of the North
  and the West.

VII.

Then swiftly the quick-breathing city,
The fearful and panic-struck city,
The startled and fire-deluged city,
Rushed back from the South and the West.
And loudly the fire-bells were clanging, and ringing their funeral notes;
And loudly wild accents of terror came pealing from thousands of throats;
And loud was the wagon's deep rumbling, and loud the wheel's clatter
  and creak;
And loud was the calling for succor from those who were sightless and
  weak;
And loud were the hoofs of the horses, and loud was the tramping of
  feet;
And loud was the gale's ceaseless howling through fire-lighted alley and
  street;

"AND LOUDLY WILD ACCENTS OF TERROR CAME PEALING FROM THOUSANDS OF THROATS."

But louder, yet louder, the crashing of roofs and of walls as they fell;
And louder, yet louder, the roaring that told of the coming of hell.
The Fire-king threw back his black mantle from off his great blood-
    dappled breast,
And sneered in the face of Chicago, the Queen of the North and the
    West.

VIII.

And there, in the terrible city,
The panic-struck, terror-crazed city,
The flying and flame-pursued city,
The torch of the North and the West,
A beautiful maiden lay moaning, as many a day she had lain,
In fetters of wearisome weakness, and throbbings of pitiful pain.
The amorous Fire-king came to her—he breathed his hot breath on her
    cheek;
She fled from his touch, but he caught her, and held her, all pulseless
    and weak.
The Fire-king he caught her and held her, in warm and unyielding em-
    brace;
He wrapped her about in his vestments, he pressed his hot lips to her face;
Then, sated and palled with his triumph, he scornfully flung her away,
And, blackened and crushed in the ruins, unknown and uncoffined, she
    lay—
Lay, blackened and crushed by the Fire-king, in ruined and desolate rest,
Like ravished and ruined Chicago, the Queen of the North and the West.

IX.

'Twas morn in the desolate city,
The ragged and ruin-heaped city,
The homeless and hot-smoking city,
The grief of the North and the West.
But down from the West came the bidding, "O Queen, lift in courage
    thy head!
Thy friends and thy neighbors awaken, and hasten, with raiment and
    bread."

And up from the South came the bidding, "Cheer up, fairest Queen of
  the Lakes!
For comfort and aid shall be coming from out our savannas and brakes!"
And down from the North came the bidding, "O city, be hopeful of
  cheer!
We've somewhat to spare for thy sufferers, for all of our suffering here!"
And up from the East came the bidding, "O city, be dauntless and bold!
Look hither for food and for raiment—look hither for credit and gold!"
And all through the world went the bidding, "Bring hither your choicest
  and best,
For weary and hungry Chicago, sad Queen of the North and the West!"

X.

O crushed but invincible city!
O broken but fast-rising city!
O glorious and unconquered city,
  Still Queen of the North and the West!
The long, golden years of the future, with treasures increasing and rare,
Shall glisten upon thy rich garments, shall twine in the folds of thy hair!
From out the black heaps of thy ruins new columns of beauty shall rise,
And glittering domes shall fling grandly our nation's proud flag to the
  skies!
From off thy wide prairies of splendor the treasures of autumn shall
  pour,
The breezes shall sweep from the northward, and hurry the ships to thy
  shore!
For Heaven will look downward in mercy on those who've passed under
  the rod,
And happ'ly again they will prosper, and bask in the blessings of God.
Once more thou shalt stand mid the cities, by prosperous breezes caressed,
O grand and unconquered Chicago, still Queen of the North and the
  West!

THE RAILROAD HOLOCAUST.

[NEW HAMBURG, N. Y., FEBRUARY, 1871.]

OVER the length of the beaten track,
Into the darkness deep and black,
　　Heavy and fast
　　As a mountain blast,
With scream of whistle and clang of gong,
The great train rattled and thundered along.

Travelers, cushioned and sheltered, sat,
Passing the time with doze and chat;
　　Thinking of naught
　　With danger fraught;
Whiling the hours with whim and song,
As the great train rattled and thundered along.

Covered and still the sleepers lay,
Lost to the dangers of the way;
　　Wandering back,
　　Adown life's track,
A thousand dreamy scenes among;
And the great train rattled and thundered along.

Heavily breathed the man of care;
Lightly slept the maiden fair;
　　And the mother pressed
　　Unto her breast
Her beautiful babes, with yearning strong;
And the great train rattled and thundered along.

Shading his eyes with his brawny hand,
Danger ahead the driver scanned;
　　And he turned the steam,
　　For the red light's gleam

Flashed warning to him there was something wrong;
But the great train rattled and thundered along.

"Down the brakes!" rang the driver's shout:
"Down the brakes!" sang the whistle out:
        But the speed was high,
        And the danger nigh,
And Death was waiting to build his pyre;
And the train dashed into a river of fire.

Into the night the red flames gleamed;
High they leaped and crackled and streamed;
        And the great train loomed,
        Like a monster doomed,
In the midst of the flames and their ruthless ire—
In the murderous tide of a river of fire.

Roused the sleeper within his bed;
A crash, a plunge, and a gleam of red,
        And the sweltering heat
        Of his winding-sheet
Clung round his form, with an agony dire;
And he moaned and died in a river of fire.

And they who were spared from the fearful death,
Thanked God for life, with quickened breath,
        And groaned that, too late,
        From a terrible fate
To rescue their comrades was their desire,
Ere they sunk in a river of death and fire.

Pity for them who, helpless, died,
And sunk in the river's merciless tide;
        And blessings infold
        The driver bold,
Who, daring for honor, and not for hire,
Went down with his train in the river of fire.

THE CABLE.

PEAL the clanging bell!
   Thunder the brazen gun!
Over the earth in triumph swell
   The notes of a victory won!
Not over field and ditch and corse;
Not by musketry, cannon, and horse;
Not by skirmishes bloody and fell;
Not by the whiz of shot and shell;
   But men of will and thought,
     Men of muscle and brain,
   Have planned, and toiled, and suffered, and fought,
     And conquered the raging main!

Far from an Eastern shore,
   By the second ark is brought,
Spanning the dusky distance o'er,
   A line of glowing thought!
Dashing through ripples and torrents and waves,
Courting the gloom of mariners' graves;
Hastily threading the ocean aisles,
And bringing to naught three thousand miles!
   For men of will and thought,
     Men of muscle and brain,
   Have planned, and toiled, and suffered, and fought,
     And conquered the raging main!

Time in his car, indeed,
   Flits fast from place to place;
But restless Thought has dared his speed,
   And Thought has won the race!

Man is as naught in Time's fierce clasp,
But Thought can escape his greedy grasp;
And Time shall have perished, by-and-by,
But the soul of Thought can never die!
    Thunder the guns as you ought!
        Well may the church-bells chime!
    For man, with the Heaven-given sword of Thought,
        Has conquered the Scythe of Time!

SHIP "CITY OF BOSTON."

"We only know she sailed away,
And ne'er was heard of more."

WAVES of the ocean that thunder and roar,
Where is the ship that we sent from our shore?
Tell, as ye dash on the quivering strand,
Where is the crew that comes never to land?
Where are the hearts that, unfearing and gay,
Broke from the clasp of affection away?

Where are the faces that, smiling and bright,
Sailed for the death-darkened regions of night?
Waves of the ocean, that thunder and roar,
Where is the ship that we sent from our shore?

Storms of the ocean, that bellow and sweep,
Where are the friends that went forth on the deep?
Where are the faces ye paled with your sneer?
Where are the hearts ye have frozen with fear?

Where is the maiden, young, tender, and fair?
Where is the grandsire, of silvery hair?
Where is the glory of womanhood's time?
Where the warm blood of man's vigor and prime?
Storms of the ocean, that bellow and pour,
Where is the ship that we sent from our shore?

Birds of the ocean, that scream through the gale,
What have ye seen of a wind-beaten sail?
Perched ye for rest on the shivering mast,
Beaten, and shattered, and bent by the blast?
Heard ye the storm-threatened mariner's plea,
Birds of the bitter and treacherous sea?
Heard ye no message to carry away
Home to the hearts that are yearning to-day?
Birds of the ocean, that hover and soar,
Where is the ship that we sent from our shore?

Depths of the ocean, that fathomless lie,
Where is the crew that no more cometh nigh?
What of the guests that so silently sleep
Low in thy chambers, relentlessly deep?
Cold is the couch they have haplessly won;
Long is the night they have entered upon;
Still must they sleep till the trumpet o'erhead
Summons the sea to uncover its dead.
Depths of the ocean, with treasures in store,
Where is the ship that we sent from our shore?

THE GOOD OF THE FUTURE.

WHY is the mire in the trodden street,
   And the dark stream by the sewer borne,
Spurned from even under our feet,
    Grudged by us e'en the look of scorn?
       There is fresh grass in its gloom—
       There are sweetness and bloom;
       There is pulse for men to eat—
       There are golden acres of wheat.
But so it is, and hath ever been:
The good of the future is e'er unseen.

Why is the mud of humanity spurned
   E'en from the tread of the passer-by?
Why is the look of pity turned
   From the bare feet and the downcast eye?
       There is virtue yet to spring
       From this poor trodden thing;
       There are germs of godlike power
       In the trials of this hour;
But so it is, and hath ever been:
The man of the future is e'er unseen.

THE JOYS THAT ARE LEFT.

If the sun have been gone while we deemed it might shine;
If the day steal away with no hope-bearing sign;
If the night, with no sight of its stars or its moon,
But such clouds as it hath, closes down on our path over-dark and o'er-
    soon;

If a voice we rejoice in its sweetness to hear,
Breathe a strain for our pain that glides back to our ear;
If a friend mark the end of a page that was bright,
Without pretext or need, by some reptile-like deed that coils plain in
    our sight;

If life's charms in our arms grow a-tired and take wing;
If the flowers that are ours turn to nettles and sting;
If the home sink in gloom that we labored to save,
And the garden we trained, when its best bloom is gained, be enriched
    by a grave;

Shall we deem that life's dream is a toil and a snare?
Shall we lie down and die on the couch of despair?
Shall we throw needless woe on our sad heart bereft?
Or, grown tearfully wise, look with pain-chastened eyes at the joys that
    are left?

For the tree that we see on the landscape so fair,
When we hie to it nigh, may be fruitless and bare;
While the vine that doth twine 'neath the blades of the grass,
With sweet nourishment rife, holds the chalice of life toward our lips as
    we pass.

So with hope let us grope for what joys we may find;
Let not fears, let not tears make us heedless or blind;
Let us think, while we drink the sweet pleasures that are,
That in sea or in ground many gems may be found that outdazzle the
  star.

There be deeds may fill needs we have suffered in vain,
There be smiles whose pure wiles may yet banish our pain,
And the heaven to us given may be found ere we die;
For God's glory and grace, and His great holy place, are not all in the
  sky.

VALUABLE & INTERESTING WORKS

VALUABLE & INTERESTING WORKS

FOR PUBLIC AND PRIVATE LIBRARIES,

Published by HARPER & BROTHERS, New York.

☞ *For a full List of Books suitable for Libraries, see* HARPER & BROTHERS' TRADE-LIST *and* CATALOGUE, *which may be had gratuitously on application to the Publishers personally, or by letter enclosing Ten Cents.*

☞ HARPER & BROTHERS *will send any of the following works by mail, postage prepaid, to any part of the United States or Canada, on receipt of the price.*

MOTLEY'S DUTCH REPUBLIC. The Rise of the Dutch Republic. A History. By JOHN LOTHROP MOTLEY, LL.D., D.C.L. With a Portrait of William of Orange. 3 vols., 8vo, Cloth, $10 50; Sheep, $12 00; Half Calf, Extra, $17 25.

MOTLEY'S UNITED NETHERLANDS. History of the United Netherlands: from the Death of William the Silent to the Twelve Years' Truce. With a full View of the English-Dutch Struggle against Spain, and of the Origin and Destruction of the Spanish Armada. By JOHN LOTHROP MOTLEY, LL.D., D.C.L. Portraits. 4 vols., 8vo, Cloth, $14 00; Sheep, $16 00; Half Calf, Extra, $23 00.

MOTLEY'S LIFE AND DEATH OF JOHN OF BARNEVELD. Life and Death of John of Barneveld, Advocate of Holland. With a View of the Primary Causes and Movements of "The Thirty-Years' War." By JOHN LOTHROP MOTLEY, D.C.L. With Illustrations. 2 vols., 8vo, Cloth, $7 00; Sheep, $8 00; Half Calf, $11 50.

TRISTRAM'S LAND OF MOAB. The Land of Moab: The Result of Travels and Discoveries on the East Side of the Dead Sea and the Jordan. By H. B. TRISTRAM, M.A., LL.D., F.R.S. With a Chapter on the Persian Palace of Mashita, by JAS. FERGUSON, F.R.S. With Maps and Ill's. Crown 8vo, Cloth, $2 50.

SCHWEINFURTH'S HEART OF AFRICA. The Heart of Africa; or, Three Years' Travels and Adventures in the Unexplored Regions of the Centre of Africa. From 1868 to 1871. By Dr. GEORG SCHWEINFURTH. Translated by ELLEN E. FREWER. With an Introduction by WINWOOD READE. Illustrated by about 130 Woodcuts from Drawings made by the Author, and with two Maps. 2 vols., 8vo, Cloth, $8 00.

FLAMMARION'S ATMOSPHERE. The Atmosphere. Translated from the French of CAMILLE FLAMMARION. Edited by JAMES GLAISHER, F.R.S., Superintendent of the Magnetical and Meteorological Department of the Royal Observatory at Greenwich. With 10 Chromo-Lithographs and 86 Woodcuts. 8vo, Cloth, $6 00.

EVANGELICAL ALLIANCE CONFERENCE, 1873. History, Essays, Orations, and Other Documents of the Sixth General Conference of the Evangelical Alliance, held in New York Oct. 2-12, 1873. Edited by Rev. PHILIP SCHAFF, D.D., and Rev. S. IRENÆUS PRIME, D.D. With Portraits of Rev. Messrs. Pronier, Carrasco, and Cook, recently deceased. 8vo, Cloth, nearly 800 pages, $6 00.

SANTO DOMINGO, Past and Present: with a Glance at Hayti. By SAMUEL HAZARD. Maps and Illustrations. Crown 8vo, Cloth, $3 50.

BALDWIN'S PRE-HISTORIC NATIONS. Pre-Historic Nations; or, Inquiries concerning some of the Great Peoples and Civilizations of Antiquity, and their Probable Relation to a still Older Civilization of the Ethiopians or Cushites of Arabia. By JOHN D. BALDWIN, Member of the American Oriental Society. 12mo, Cloth, $1 75.

DRAKE'S NOOKS AND CORNERS OF THE NEW ENGLAND COAST. Nooks and Corners of the New England Coast. By SAMUEL ADAMS DRAKE, Author of "Old Landmarks of Boston," "Historic Fields and Mansions of Middlesex," &c. With numerous Illustrations. 8vo, Cloth, $3 50.

GREEN'S SHORT HISTORY OF THE ENGLISH PEOPLE. A Short History of the English People. By J. R. GREEN, M.A., Examiner in the School of Modern History, Oxford. With Tables and Colored Maps. 8vo, Cloth, $1 75.

MOHAMMED AND MOHAMMEDANISM: Lectures Delivered at the Royal Institution of Great Britain in February and March, 1874. By R. BOSWORTH SMITH, M.A., Assistant Master in Harrow School; late Fellow of Trinity College, Oxford. With an Appendix containing Emanuel Deutsch's Article on "Islam." 12mo, Cloth, $1 50.

POETS OF THE NINETEENTH CENTURY. The Poets of the Nineteenth Century. Selected and Edited by the Rev. ROBERT ARIS WILLMOTT. With English and American Additions, arranged by EVERT A. DUYCKINCK, Editor of "Cyclopædia of American Literature." Comprising Selections from the Greatest Authors of the Age. Superbly Illustrated with 141 Engravings from Designs by the most Eminent Artists. New and Enlarged Edition. In elegant Square 8vo form, printed on Superfine Tinted Paper, richly bound in extra Cloth, Beveled, Gilt Edges, $5 00; Half Calf, $5 50; Full Turkey Morocco, $9 00.

THE REVISION OF THE ENGLISH VERSION OF THE NEW TESTAMENT. By LIGHTFOOT, TRENCH, and ELLICOTT. With an Introduction by the Rev. P. SCHAFF, D.D. 618 pp., Crown 8vo, Cloth, $3 00.
This work embraces in one volume:
I. ON A FRESH REVISION OF THE ENGLISH NEW TESTAMENT. By J. B. LIGHTFOOT, D.D., Canon of St. Paul's, and Hulsean Professor of Divinity, Cambridge. Second Edition, Revised. 196 pp.
II. ON THE AUTHORIZED VERSION OF THE NEW TESTAMENT in Connection with some Recent Proposals for its Revision. By RICHARD CHENEVIX TRENCH, D.D., Archbishop of Dublin. 194 pp.
III. CONSIDERATIONS ON THE REVISION OF THE ENGLISH VERSION OF THE NEW TESTAMENT. By J. C. ELLICOTT, D.D., Bishop of Gloucester and Bristol. 178 pp.

ADDISON'S COMPLETE WORKS. The Works of Joseph Addison, embracing the whole of the "Spectator." Complete in 3 vols., 8vo, Cloth, $6 00.

SIR SAMUEL BAKER'S ISMAILÏA. Ismailïa: A Narrative of the Expedition to Central Africa for the Suppression of the Slave Trade. Organized by ISMAIL, Khedive of Egypt. By Sir SAMUEL W. BAKER, Pasha, M.A., F.R.S., F.R.G.S. With Maps, Portraits, and upward of Fifty full-page Illustrations by ZWECKER and DURAND. 8vo, Cloth, $5 00.

NORDHOFF'S CALIFORNIA. California: for Health, Pleasure, and Residence. A Book for Travellers and Settlers. By CHARLES NORDHOFF. With Illustrations. 8vo, Cloth, $2 50.

NORDHOFF'S NORTHERN CALIFORNIA, ORE-GON, AND THE SANDWICH ISLANDS. Northern California, Oregon, and the Sandwich Islands. By CHARLES NORDHOFF. Profusely Illustrated. 8vo, Cloth, $2 50.

NORDHOFF'S 'COMMUNISTIC SOCIETIES OF THE UNITED STATES. The Communistic Societies of the United States; from Personal Visit and Observation: including Detailed Accounts of the Economists, Zoarites, Shakers, the Amana, Oneida, Bethel, Aurora, Icarian, and Other Existing Societies, their Religious Creeds, Social Practices, Numbers, Industries, and Present Condition. By CHARLES NORDHOFF. With Illustrations. 8vo, Cloth, $4 00.

VINCENT'S LAND OF THE WHITE ELEPHANT. The Land of the White Elephant. Sights and Scenes in Southeastern Asia. A Personal Narrative of Travel and Adventure in Farther India, embracing the Countries of Burma, Siam, Cambodia, and Cochin-China (1871-2). By FRANK VINCENT, Jr. With Map, Plans, and numerous Illustrations. Crown 8vo, Cloth, $3 50.

MYERS'S REMAINS OF LOST EMPIRES. Remains of Lost Empires. Sketches of the Ruins of Palmyra, Nineveh, Babylon, and Persepolis, with some Notes on India and the Cashmerian Himalayas. By P.V.N. MYERS, A.M. Illustrations. 8vo, Cloth, $3 50.

HAYDN'S DICTIONARY OF DATES, relating to all Ages and Nations. For Universal Reference. Edited by BENJAMIN VINCENT, Assistant Secretary and Keeper of the Library of the Royal Institution of Great Britain; and Revised for the Use of American Readers. 8vo, Cloth, $5 00; Sheep, $6 00.

MACGREGOR'S ROB ROY ON THE JORDAN. The Rob Roy on the Jordan, Nile, Red Sea, and Gennesareth, &c. A Canoe Cruise in Palestine and Egypt, and the Waters of Damascus. By J. MAC-GREGOR, M.A. With Maps and Illustrations. Crown 8vo, Cloth, $2 50.

WALLACE'S MALAY ARCHIPELAGO. The Malay Archipelago: the Land of the Orang-Utan, and the Bird of Paradise. A Narrative of Travel, 1854-'62. With Studies of Man and Nature. By ALFRED RUS-SEL WALLACE. With Maps and numerous Illustrations. Crown 8vo, Cloth, $2 50.

WHYMPER'S ALASKA. Travel and Adventure in the Territory of Alaska, formerly Russian America —now Ceded to the United States—and in various other Parts of the North Pacific. By FREDERICK WHYMPER. With Map and Illustrations. Crown 8vo, Cloth, $2 50.

ORTON'S ANDES AND THE AMAZON. The Andes and the Amazon; or, Across the Continent of South America. By JAMES ORTON, M.A., Professor of Natural History in Vassar College, Poughkeepsie, N. Y., and Corresponding Member of the Academy of Natural Sciences, Philadelphia. With a New Map of Equatorial America and numerous Illustrations. Crown 8vo, Cloth, $2 00.

WINCHELL'S SKETCHES OF CREATION. Sketches of Creation: a Popular View of some of the Grand Conclusions of the Sciences in reference to the History of Matter and of Life. Together with a Statement of the Intimations of Science respecting the Primordial Condition and the Ultimate Destiny of the Earth and the Solar System. By ALEXANDER WINCHELL, LL.D. With Illustrations. 12mo, Cloth, $2 00.

WHITE'S MASSACRE OF ST. BARTHOLOMEW. The Massacre of St. Bartholomew: Preceded by a History of the Religious Wars in the Reign of Charles IX. By HENRY WHITE, M.A. With Illustrations. 8vo, Cloth, $1 75.

LOSSING'S FIELD-BOOK OF THE REVOLUTION. Pictorial Field-Book of the Revolution; or, Illustrations by Pen and Pencil of the History, Biography, Scenery, Relics, and Traditions of the War for Independence. By BENSON J. LOSSING. 2 vols., 8vo, Cloth, $14 00; Sheep, $15 00; Half Calf, $18 00; Full Turkey Morocco, Gilt Edges, $22 00.

LOSSING'S FIELD-BOOK OF THE WAR OF 1812. Pictorial Field-Book of the War of 1812; or, Illustrations by Pen and Pencil of the History, Biography, Scenery, Relics, and Traditions of the last War for American Independence. By BENSON J. LOS-SING. With 882 Illustrations, engraved on Wood by Lossing & Barritt, chiefly from Original Sketches by the Author. Complete in One Volume, 1084 pages, large 8vo. Price, in Cloth, $7 00; Sheep, $8 50; Full Roan, $9 00; Half Calf or Half Morocco extra, $10 00; Full Morocco, Gilt Edges, $12 00.

ALFORD'S GREEK TESTAMENT. The Greek Testament: with a critically revised Text; a Digest of Various Readings; Marginal References to Verbal and Idiomatic Usage; Prolegomena; and a Critical and Exegetical Commentary. For the Use of Theological Students and Ministers. By HENRY ALFORD, D.D., Dean of Canterbury. Vol. I., containing the Four Gospels. 944 pages, 8vo, Cloth, $6 00; Sheep, $6 50.

ABBOTT'S FREDERICK THE GREAT. The History of Frederick the Second, called Frederick the Great. By JOHN S. C. ABBOTT. Elegantly Illustrated. 8vo, Cloth, $5 00.

ABBOTT'S HISTORY OF THE FRENCH REVOLUTION. The French Revolution of 1789, as viewed in the Light of Republican Institutions. By JOHN S. C. ABBOTT. With 100 Engravings. 8vo, Cloth, $5 00.

ABBOTT'S NAPOLEON BONAPARTE. The History of Napoleon Bonaparte. By JOHN S. C. AB-BOTT. With Maps, Woodcuts, and Portraits on Steel. 2 vols., 8vo, Cloth, $10 00.

ABBOTT'S NAPOLEON AT ST. HELENA; or, Interesting Anecdotes and Remarkable Conversations of the Emperor during the Five and a Half Years of his Captivity. Collected from the Memorials of Las Casas, O'Meara, Montholon, Antommarchi, and others. By JOHN S. C. ABBOTT. With Illustrations. 8vo, Cloth, $5 00.

ALCOCK'S JAPAN. The Capital of the Tycoon: a Narrative of a Three Years' Residence in Japan. By Sir RUTHERFORD ALCOCK, K.C.B., Her Majesty's Envoy Extraordinary and Minister Plenipotentiary in Japan. With Maps and Engravings. 2 vols., 12mo, Cloth, $3 50.

ALISON'S HISTORY OF EUROPE. FIRST SERIES: From the Commencement of the French Revolution, in 1789, to the Restoration of the Bourbons, in 1815. [In addition to the Notes on Chapter LXXVI., which correct the errors of the original work concerning the United States, a copious Analytical Index has been appended to this American edition.] SECOND SERIES: From the Fall of Napoleon, in 1815, to the Accession of Louis Napoleon, in 1852. 8 vols., 8vo, Cloth, $16 00.

BARTH'S NORTH AND CENTRAL AFRICA. Travels and Discoveries in North and Central Africa. Being a Journal of an Expedition undertaken under the Auspices of H.B.M.'s Government in the Years 1849-1855. By HENRY BARTH, Ph.D., D.C.L. Illustrated. 3 vols., 8vo, Cloth, $12 00.

BRODHEAD'S HISTORY OF NEW YORK. History of the State of New York. By JOHN ROMEYN BRODHEAD. 1609-1691. Two Vols. 8vo, Cloth, $3 00 per vol.

BOSWELL'S JOHNSON. The Life of Samuel Johnson, LL.D. Including a Journey to the Hebrides. By JAMES BOSWELL, Esq. A New Edition, with numerous Additions and Notes. By JOHN WILSON CROKER, LL.D., F.R.S. Portrait of Boswell. 2 vols., 8vo, Cloth, $4 00.

HENRY WARD BEECHER'S SERMONS. Sermons by HENRY WARD BEECHER, Plymouth Church, Brooklyn. Selected from Published and Unpublished Discourses, and Revised by their Author. With Steel Portrait. Complete in 2 vols., 8vo, Cloth, $5 00.

LYMAN BEECHER'S AUTOBIOGRAPHY, &c. Autobiography, Correspondence, &c., of Lyman Beecher, D.D. Edited by his Son, CHARLES BEECHER. With Three Steel Portraits and Engravings on Wood. 2 vols., 12mo, Cloth, $5 00.

DRAPER'S CIVIL WAR. History of the American Civil War. By JOHN W. DRAPER, M.D., LL.D., Professor of Chemistry and Physiology in the University of New York. In Three Vols. 8vo, Cloth, $3 50 per vol.

DRAPER'S INTELLECTUAL DEVELOPMENT OF EUROPE. A History of the Intellectual Development of Europe. By JOHN W. DRAPER, M.D., LL.D., Professor of Chemistry and Physiology in the University of New York. 8vo, Cloth, $5 00.

DRAPER'S AMERICAN CIVIL POLICY. Thoughts on the Future Civil Policy of America. By JOHN W. DRAPER, M.D., LL.D., Professor of Chemistry and Physiology in the University of New York. Crown 8vo, Cloth, $2 50.

DU CHAILLU'S AFRICA. Explorations and Adventures in Equatorial Africa ; with Accounts of the Manners and Customs of the People, and of the Chase of the Gorilla, the Crocodile, Leopard, Elephant, Hippopotamus, and other Animals. By PAUL B. DU CHAILLU. Numerous Illustrations. 8vo, Cloth, $5 00.

DU CHAILLU'S ASHANGO LAND. A Journey to Ashango Land, and Further Penetration into Equatorial Africa. By PAUL B. DU CHAILLU. New Edition. Handsomely Illustrated. 8vo, Cloth, $5 00.

BROUGHAM'S AUTOBIOGRAPHY. Life and Times of HENRY, LORD BROUGHAM. Written by Himself. In Three Volumes. 12mo, Cloth, $2 00 per vol.

BULWER'S ESSAYS. Miscellaneous Prose Works of Edward Bulwer, Lord Lytton, including "Caxtoniana." 3 vols., 12mo, Cloth, $5 25.

BULWER'S HORACE. The Odes and Epodes of Horace. A Metrical Translation into English. With Introduction and Commentaries. By LORD LYTTON. With Latin Text from the Editions of Orelli, Macleane, and Yonge. 12mo, Cloth, $1 75.

BULWER'S KING ARTHUR. A Poem. By EARL LYTTON. New Edition. 12mo, Cloth, $1 75.

BURNS'S LIFE AND WORKS. The Life and Works of Robert Burns. Edited by ROBERT CHAMBERS. 4 vols., 12mo, Cloth, $6 00.

CARLYLE'S FREDERICK THE GREAT. History of Friedrich II., called Frederick the Great. By THOMAS CARLYLE. Portraits, Maps, Plans, &c. 6 vols., 12mo, Cloth, $12 00.

CARLYLE'S FRENCH REVOLUTION. History of the French Revolution. Newly Revised by the Author, with Index, &c. 2 vols., 12mo, Cloth, $3 50.

CARLYLE'S OLIVER CROMWELL. Letters and Speeches of Oliver Cromwell. With Elucidations and Connecting Narrative. 2 vols.,12mo,Cloth, $3 50.

CHALMERS'S POSTHUMOUS WORKS. The Posthumous Works of Dr. Chalmers. Edited by his Son-in-Law, Rev. WILLIAM HANNA, LL.D. Complete in 9 vols., 12mo, Cloth, $13 50.

DOOLITTLE'S CHINA. Social Life of the Chinese: with some Account of their Religious, Governmental, Educational, and Business Customs and Opinions. With special but not exclusive Reference to Fuhchau. By Rev. JUSTUS DOOLITTLE, Fourteen Years Member of the Fuhchau Mission of the American Board. Illustrated with more than 150 characteristic Engravings on Wood. 2 vols., 12mo, Cloth, $5 00.

GIBBON'S ROME. History of the Decline and Fall of the Roman Empire. By EDWARD GIBBON. With Notes by Rev. H. H. MILMAN and M. GUIZOT. A new Cheap Edition. To which is added a complete Index of the whole Work, and a Portrait of the Author. 6 vols., 12mo, Cloth, $9 00.

HARPER'S NEW CLASSICAL LIBRARY. Literal Translations.
The following Volumes are now ready. Portraits. 12mo, Cloth, $1 50 each.
CÆSAR.—VIRGIL.—SALLUST.—HORACE.—CICERO'S ORATIONS.—CICERO'S OFFICES, &c.—CICERO ON ORATORY AND ORATORS.—TACITUS (2 vols.).—TERENCE. — SOPHOCLES. — JUVENAL. — XENOPHON.—HOMER'S ILIAD.—HOMER'S ODYSSEY. — HERODOTUS.—DEMOSTHENES.—THUCYDIDES.—ÆSCHYLUS.—EURIPIDES (2 vols.).—LIVY (2 vols.).—PLATO.

EDGEWORTH'S (MISS) NOVELS. With Engravings. 10 vols., 12mo, Cloth, $15 00.

GROTE'S HISTORY OF GREECE. 12 vols., 12mo, Cloth, $18 00.

HELPS'S SPANISH CONQUEST. The Spanish Conquest in America, and its Relation to the History of Slavery and to the Government of Colonies. By ARTHUR HELPS. 4 vols., 12mo, Cloth, $6 00.

HALE'S (MRS.) WOMAN'S RECORD. Woman's Record ; or, Biographical Sketches of all Distinguished Women, from the Creation to the Present Time. Arranged in Four Eras, with Selections from Female Writers of each Era. By MRS. SARAH JOSEPHA HALE. Illustrated with more than 200 Portraits. 8vo, Cloth, $5 00.

HALL'S ARCTIC RESEARCHES. Arctic Researches and Life among the Esquimaux : being the Narrative of an Expedition in Search of Sir John Franklin, in the Years 1860, 1861, and 1862. By CHARLES FRANCIS HALL. With Maps and 100 Illustrations. The Illustrations are from Original Drawings by Charles Parsons, Henry L. Stephens, Solomon Eytinge, W. S. L. Jewett, and Granville Perkins, after Sketches by Captain Hall. 8vo, Cloth, $5 00.

HALLAM'S CONSTITUTIONAL HISTORY OF ENGLAND, from the Accession of Henry VII. to the Death of George II. 8vo, Cloth, $2 00.

HALLAM'S LITERATURE. Introduction to the Literature of Europe during the Fifteenth, Sixteenth, and Seventeenth Centuries. By HENRY HALLAM. 2 vols., 8vo, Cloth, $4 00.

HALLAM'S MIDDLE AGES. State of Europe during the Middle Ages. By HENRY HALLAM. 8vo, Cloth, $2 00.

HILDRETH'S HISTORY OF THE UNITED STATES. FIRST SERIES: From the First Settlement of the Country to the Adoption of the Federal Constitution. SECOND SERIES: From the Adoption of the Federal Constitution to the End of the Sixteenth Congress. 6 vols., 8vo, Cloth, $18 00.

HUME'S HISTORY OF ENGLAND. History of England, from the Invasion of Julius Cæsar to the Abdication of James II., 1688. By DAVID HUME. With the Author's Last Corrections and Improvements. To which is prefixed a short Account of his Life, written by himself. 6 vols., 12mo, Cloth, $9 00 ; Sheep, $11 40 ; Half Calf, $19 50.

JOHNSON'S COMPLETE WORKS. The Works of Samuel Johnson, LL.D. With an Essay on his Life and Genius, by ARTHUR MURPHY, Esq. Portrait of Johnson. 2 vols., 8vo, Cloth, $4 00.

KINGLAKE'S CRIMEAN WAR. The Invasion of the Crimea, and an Account of its Progress down to the Death of Lord Raglan. By ALEXANDER WILLIAM KINGLAKE. With Maps and Plans. Three Vols. ready. 12mo, Cloth, $2 00 per vol.

KINGSLEY'S WEST INDIES. The West Indies. At Last: A Christmas in the West Indies. By the Rev. CHARLES KINGSLEY. Illustrated. 12mo, Cloth, $1 50.

LAMB'S COMPLETE WORKS. The Works of Charles Lamb. Comprising his Letters, Poems, Essays of Elia, Essays upon Shakspeare, Hogarth, &c., and a Sketch of his Life, with the Final Memorials, by T. Noon Talfourd. Portrait. 2 vols., 12mo, Cloth, $3 00.

LIVINGSTONE'S SOUTH AFRICA. Missionary Travels and Researches in South Africa; including a Sketch of Sixteen Years' Residence in the Interior of Africa, and a Journey from the Cape of Good Hope to Loando on the West Coast; thence across the Continent, down the River Zambesi, to the Eastern Ocean. By David Livingstone, LL.D., D.C.L. With Portrait, Maps by Arrowsmith, and numerous Illustrations. 8vo, Cloth, $4 50.

LIVINGSTONE'S ZAMBESI. Narrative of an Expedition to the Zambesi and its Tributaries, and of the Discovery of the Lakes Shirwa and Nyassa, 1858-1864. By David and Charles Livingstone. With Map and Illustrations. 8vo, Cloth, $5 00.

DR. LIVINGSTONE'S LAST JOURNALS. The Last Journals of Dr. Livingstone in Central Africa, from 1865 to his Death. Continued by a Narrative of his Last Moments and Sufferings, obtained from his Faithful Servants Chuma and Susi. By Horace Waller, F.R.G.S., Rector of Twywell, Northampton. With Maps and Illustrations. 8vo, Cloth, $5 00. Cheap Edition, with Map and Illustrations, 8vo, Cloth, $2 50.

M'CLINTOCK & STRONG'S CYCLOPÆDIA. Cyclopædia of Biblical, Theological, and Ecclesiastical Literature. Prepared by the Rev. John M'Clintock, D.D., and James Strong, S.T.D. 5 vols. now ready. Royal 8vo. Price per vol., Cloth, $5 00; Sheep, $6 00; Half Morocco, $8 00.

RECLUS'S EARTH. The Earth: a Descriptive History of the Phenomena of the Life of the Globe. By Elisée Reclus. Translated by the late B. B. Woodward, and Edited by Henry Woodward. With 234 Maps and Illustrations, and 23 Page Maps printed in Colors. Second American Edition, with copious Index. 8vo, Cloth, $5 00.

RECLUS'S OCEAN. The Ocean, Atmosphere, and Life. Being the Second Series of a Descriptive History of the Life of the Globe. By Elisée Reclus. Translated. Illustrated with 250 Maps or Figures, and 27 Maps printed in Colors. 8vo, Cloth, $6 00.

SHAKSPEARE. The Dramatic Works of William Shakspeare, with the Corrections and Illustrations of Dr. Johnson, G. Steevens, and others. Revised by Isaac Reed. Engravings. 6 vols., Royal 12mo, Cloth, $9 00.

SMILES'S LIFE OF THE STEPHENSONS. The Life of George Stephenson, and of his Son, Robert Stephenson; comprising, also, a History of the Invention and Introduction of the Railway Locomotive. By Samuel Smiles. With Steel Portraits and numerous Illustrations. 8vo, Cloth, $3 00.

SMILES'S HISTORY OF THE HUGUENOTS. The Huguenots: their Settlements, Churches, and Industries in England and Ireland. By Samuel Smiles. With an Appendix relating to the Huguenots in America. Crown 8vo, Cloth, $1 75.

SMILES'S HUGUENOTS AFTER THE REVOCATION. The Huguenots in France after the Revocation of the Edict of Nantes; with a Visit to the Country of the Vaudois. By Samuel Smiles. Crown 8vo, Cloth, $2 00.

SPEKE'S AFRICA. Journal of the Discovery of the Source of the Nile. By Captain John Hanning Speke. With Maps and Portraits and numerous Illustrations, chiefly from Drawings by Captain Grant. 8vo, Cloth, uniform with Livingstone, Barth, Burton, &c., $4 00.

STRICKLAND'S (Miss) QUEENS OF SCOTLAND. Lives of the Queens of Scotland and English Princesses connected with the Regal Succession of Great Britain. By Agnes Strickland. 8 vols., 12mo, Cloth, $12 00.

THE STUDENT'S SERIES. 12mo, Cloth, $2 00 per vol.
France. Engravings.
Gibbon. Engravings.
Greece. Engravings.
Hume. Engravings.
Rome. By Liddell. Engravings.
Old Testament History. Engravings.
New Testament History. Engravings.
Strickland's Queens of England. Abridged. Engravings.
Ancient History of the East. Engravings.
Hallam's Middle Ages.
Hallam's Constitutional History of England.
Lyell's Elements of Geology. Engravings.

TENNYSON'S COMPLETE POEMS. The Complete Poems of Alfred Tennyson, Poet Laureate. With numerous Illustrations by Eminent Artists, and Three Characteristic Portraits. 8vo, Paper, 75 cents; Cloth, $1 25.

THOMSON'S LAND AND BOOK. The Land and the Book; or, Biblical Illustrations drawn from the Manners and Customs, the Scenes and the Scenery of the Holy Land. By W. M. Thomson, D.D., Twenty-five Years a Missionary of the A.B.C.F.M. in Syria and Palestine. With Two elaborate Maps of Palestine, an accurate Plan of Jerusalem, and Several Hundred Engravings, representing the Scenery Topography, and Productions of the Holy Land, and the Costumes, Manners, and Habits of the People. Two large 12mo Volumes, Cloth, $5 00.

TYERMAN'S WESLEY. The Life and Times of the Rev. John Wesley, M.A., Founder of the Methodists. By the Rev. Luke Tyerman, Author of "The Life of Rev. Samuel Wesley." Portraits. Three Vols. Crown 8vo, Cloth, $2 50 per vol.

TYERMAN'S OXFORD METHODISTS. The Oxford Methodists: Memoirs of the Rev. Messrs. Clayton, Ingham, Gambold, Hervey, and Broughton, with Biographical Notices of others. By Rev. Luke Tyerman. With Portraits. Crown 8vo, Cloth, $2 50.

TYSON'S ARCTIC EXPERIENCES. Arctic Experiences: containing Captain George E. Tyson's Drift on the Ice-Floe, a History of the Polaris Expedition, the Cruise of the Tigris, and Rescue of the Polaris Survivors. To which is added a General Arctic Chronology. Edited by E. Vale Blake. With Map and numerous Illustrations. 8vo, Cloth, $4 00.

RAWLINSON'S MANUAL OF ANCIENT HISTORY. A Manual of Ancient History, from the Earliest Times to the Fall of the Western Empire. Comprising the History of Chaldæa, Assyria, Media, Babylonia, Lydia, Phœnicia, Syria, Judæa, Egypt, Carthage, Persia, Greece, Macedonia, Parthia, and Rome. By George Rawlinson, M.A., Camden Professor of Ancient History in the University of Oxford. 12mo, Cloth, $2 50.

WOOD'S HOMES WITHOUT HANDS. Homes Without Hands: being a Description of the Habitations of Animals, classed according to their Principle of Construction. By J. G. Wood, M.A., F.L.S. With about 140 Illustrations. 8vo, Cloth, Beveled Edges, $4 50.

BELLOWS'S TRAVELS. The Old World in its New Face: Impressions of Europe in 1867, 1868. By Henry W. Bellows. 2 vols., 12mo, Cloth, $3 50.

HAZEN'S SCHOOL AND THE ARMY IN GERMANY AND FRANCE. The School and the Army in Germany and France, with a Diary of Siege Life at Versailles. By Brevet Major-General W. B. Hazen, U.S.A., Colonel Sixth Infantry. Crown 8vo, Cloth, $2 50.

COLERIDGE'S COMPLETE WORKS. The Complete Works of Samuel Taylor Coleridge. With an Introductory Essay upon his Philosophical and Theological Opinions. Edited by Professor Shedd. Complete in Seven Vols. With a fine Portrait. Small 8vo, Cloth, $10 50.